foundations of **Korean**

Martial Arts

Masters, Manuals & Combative Techniques

D1528249

An Anthology of Articles from the *Journal of Asian Martial Arts*

Compiled by Michael A. DeMarco, M.A.

Copyright © 2017
by Via Media Publishing Company
941 Calle Mejia #822
Santa Fe, NM 87501 USA

Articles in this anthology were originally published in the *Journal of Asian Martial Arts* and the book, *Asian Martial Arts: Constructive Thoughts & Practical Applications*. Listed according to the table of contents for this anthology:

Henning, S. (2000), Vol. 9 No. 1, pp. 8-15
Adrogué, M. (2003), Vol. 12 No. 4, pp. 8-33
Della Pia, J. (1994), Vol. 3 No. 2, pp. 62-71
Della Pia, J. (1995), Vol. 4 No. 2, pp. 86-97
Massey, P., & Thorner, E. (1993), Vol. 2 No. 2, pp. 70-79
Bradley, S. (2006), Vol. 15 No. 3, pp. 76-89
Tedeschi, M. (2000), Vol. 9 No. 4, pp. 76-101
Bradley, S. (2006), In *Asian Martial Arts:
Constructive Thoughts & Practical Applications*, pp. 48-51

Book and cover design
by Via Media Publishing Company

Edited by
Michael A. DeMarco, M.A.

Cover illustration

Images taken from the *Muye Dobo Tongji* (1790)
colorized for this composite.

ISBN: 978-1893765436

contents

preface

Most of what are referred to as Korean martial art styles are actually derived from Japanese/Okinawan karate systems or find their roots in Chinese boxing. The Korean peninsula has existed as a fragile territory between China and Japan and thus shared many cultural elements from their neighbors. To what degree has the Japanese and Chinese arts influenced those practiced in Korea over the centuries? Can we distinguish any original Korean martial art style?

Chapters in this anthology are derived from the *Journal of Asian Martial Arts* specifically in response to such questions as asked above. The authors provide great detail on the military/martial manuals that recorded both battlefield arts and personal combative arts and use these sources to give a picture of the martial traditions practiced in Korea for hundreds of years.

In chapter one, Stanley Henning provides an excellent overview of martial arts in Korea since the earliest dynasties. These include bare-hand arts as well as those with weaponry. His overview illuminates the time and place of highly influential military manuals as discussed in the chapter by Manuel Adrogué. John Della Pia's two chapters focus on a particular manual—the *Muye Dobo Tongji* (1790)—providing details of open-hand and weapons training, in particular with the unique Korean "native sword."

Two chapters provide the theory and practice of qigong methods for health and martial effectiveness. Dr. Patrick Massey et al. offer results on the use of breathing methods affecting lung capacity. Sean Bradley's chapter goes deeply into the medical theories that parallel the practice of Sinmoo Hapkido's qigong methods.

The final two chapters focus on practical fighting applications from Hapkido. Marc Tedeschi's chapter provides sound advice for self-defense against multiple opponents. In addition to detailing principles that give any defender a helpful advantage, Tedeschi shows nineteen examples of techniques against two, three, and four opponents that include pressure point stricking, throws, arm bars, locks, and a variety of kicks. In the closing chapter, Sean Bradley discusses a few of his favorite techniques, where he learned them, and why they are memorable.

Rich in historical details and practical advice, this anthology will prove to be a prized reference work to all interested in the Korean martial traditions.

Michael A. DeMarco, Publisher
Santa Fe, New Mexico, February 2017

chapter 1

Traditional Korean Martial Arts
by Stanley E. Henning, M.A.

Kim Keun-Hyung, Taekkyon practitioner
executing powerful kicks with grace and ease.
Photos courtesy of the Dahmul Culture Center, Seoul, Korea.

From the beginning, Korean martial arts were intertwined with those of China. Even the historical references to Korean martial arts are all in Chinese, the literary language of the Korean elites over the centuries. The earliest archaeological evidence of Korean martial arts practices (not necessarily of pure Korean origin) is found in one of a group of tombs in northeast China, an area under the Koguryo Kingdom (37 B.C.E.-668 C.E.), but colonized and under Chinese military control between 108 B.C.E. and 313 C.E. (No, 1974: 140-41; Mizuno, 1972). The wall murals at this site include one scene which clearly depicts wrestling (*juedi* in Chinese and *kakjo* in Korean) and another with two protagonists rushing at each other which has been interpreted by some as depicting boxing (*shoubo* in Chinese and *subak* in Korean). Whether or not the latter scene actually depicts boxing as opposed to wrestling remains a matter of conjecture, but what is known is that, already by this time, Chinese martial arts had developed to a relatively high degree of sophistication with a clear distinction made between wrestling and boxing practices.

Under the first Qin Dynasty (221-210 B.C.E.) emperor, wrestling was designated as the official military ceremonial activity and sport while, during the Former Han period (206 B.C.E.-24 C.E.), boxing was categorized as one of several military skills, which even included a form of football, "...to practice hand and foot movements, facilitate use of weapons, and organize for victory in offense or defense" (Chen, 1977: 2961; Gu, 1987: 205). This game of football was also adopted by the Koreans during their Three Kingdoms period (57-668), which arose toward the end of the Chinese Former Han (No, 1974: 147-158).

Left: *Liangxian*—a bamboo infantry defensive support weapon supposedly designed by general Qi Jiguang for use in small unit tactics against Japanese pirates (probably never used by Koreans). Right: Staff and flail. All illustrations are taken from *Muye Dobo Tongji* (1790, *Encyclopedia of Martial Arts Manuals*) combined with Chinese-Hangul labels. *Courtesy of S. Henning.*

In most popular Korean and English writings on the subject, the primary bit of evidence offered for the existence of a Korean form of boxing during the long period between the early cave murals and records on the Koryo period (well over 1000 years) is the presence of the stone guardian figures at the entrance to the Sokkuram Buddhist site dating to the Unified Silla period (mid-8th century). These guardians are in the style common to contemporary Tang China (618-907) on which they were most assuredly modeled. Even some reputable Korean sources refer to these figures as "wrestlers" rather than "boxers," but they are most commonly called "strong men" (*lishi* in Chinese or *ryuksa* in Korean) (Kim, 1978: 15-16; Ministry, 1956: 194-95). Some writers tend to read too much into the poses of these figures, which can be viewed as actual forms used in Chinese-style boxing, but which are primarily symbolic. The Chinese character for "fist" also meant "strength" (*quan* in Chinese, *kwon* in Korean), but did not refer to boxing in China until the Southern Song (1127-1279). There is no evidence that it was ever used to refer to boxing in Korea, until relatively recently, except in quoting Chinese sources in the

Illustrated Encyclopedia of Martial Arts Manuals (*Muye Dobo Tongji*, 1790).
Nevertheless, boxing in the form of subak almost certainly was practiced
during the Silla period (668-935). As for the often-mentioned martial arts
practices of the hwarang, a patriotic Silla period "fraternity" of youth, we have
few specifics. They are said to have practiced Confucian virtues and the
"Six Arts," which originally included archery and charioteering (they likely
substituted horsemanship and possibly other martial arts, especially swords-
manship, for charioteering, a Chinese skill which had died out long before and
which, in any case, was ill-suited to Korean terrain) (Il, 1995: 353-56; Yi, 1955:
15; Shin, 1963: 8).

Korean martial arts were probably strongly influenced by Chinese
models from the Former Han on (206 B.C.E.-24 C.E.). Although there are no
descriptive Korean references to the martial arts prior to the *Koryo History*
(completed in 1451, but covering the period 918-1392), its citations provide
evidence that the Koreans had maintained a strict distinction between
wrestling and boxing in the military, similar to the Chinese pattern, and that,
slightly different from the Chinese, they also treated boxing as a formally
recognized military sport or entertainment in a manner similar to wrestling.
This practice was continued at least into the fifteenth century as confirmed
in the *Veritable Records of the Yi Dynasty* (Yasiya, 1972; Yijo Sillok, 1953;
Gwahakwon, 1961). These records mention another military sport, also
pronounced *subak* in Korean or *shoupai* in Chinese, which was probably akin
to boxing. There are references to a similar skill, *paizhang*, during the Chinese
Southern and Northern Dynasties period (420-589). In the *Elucidation of
Names* (c. 25 CE), *pai* is defined as *bo* (as in *shoubo* or *subak*) in hitting "above"
(probably upper torso—chest and shoulders—and head) as in the Japanese
sumo technique called *tsuppari*. In at least one instance, this skill was used to
test soldiers for entry into the elite guards unit (*bangbakdae*) (Gwahakwon,
1961: 85, 210, 359; Li, 1936: 4a-4b; Liu, 1985: 2b).

Outside the military, as in China, boxing was practiced by the common
folk on festive occasions. For example, annual competitive boxing bouts were
held in the seventh month (according to the lunar calendar) in Unjin County,
near the border of North Cholla and South Chungchong Provinces, while
wrestling matches were held in a couple of locations in Seoul during the fifth
month (No, 1958: 594; Yi, 1991: 99, 225).

As with the Chinese, archery was important to the Koreans and, similar
to other groups on China's borders such as the Mongols and Manchus, the
Koreans preferred the composite bow so convenient for equestrian use (the
Chinese used the crossbow as well as the composite bow), and they practiced
archery both on foot and from horseback. Similar to the Chinese, the Koreans

also stressed use of the spear as the long weapon of choice on foot and from horseback. They bound spear tips with leather for competitive bouts. The *Veritable Records of the Yi Dynasty* also mention sword practice. Sometimes training sessions resulted in fatalities when soldiers armed with wooden spears were pitted against elite guards armed with wooden swords (Gwahakwon, 1961: 88, 99, 358, 362, 400, 405, 703).

Left: Equestrian spear. Right: Trident.

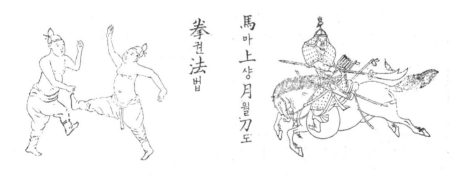

Left: Boxing (*kwonbop*) copied from General Qi Jiguang's 32 boxing forms.
Right: Equestrian crescent moon halberd.

The record becomes murky during the sixteenth century, a period characterized internally by intense factional conflicts and neglect of military affairs, and externally by increased military use of firearms in China and especially in Japan, and which culminated in turbulence caused by Japanese invasions. Then, during the end of the eighteenth century, King Jongjo displayed a renewed interest in military affairs and commissioned a book on martial skills, which was completed by Yi Dok Mu in 1790 under the title *Encyclopedia of Illustrated Martial Arts Manuals* (Yi: 1970).

Yi Dok Mu's encyclopedia offers a fairly comprehensive view of traditional Korean and Chinese martial arts practices that were, in military terms, effectively outmoded at the time of publication. It mixes research from numerous Chinese sources, including Ming general Qi Jiguang's (1528-1587) *New Book of Effective Discipline* (c. 1561), together with contemporary Korean practices, and includes illustrated routines, on foot and from horseback, for broadsword (a cross between cutlass and saber), flail, and a variety of poled weapons such as spear, trident, crescent halberd, and others. The chapter on boxing (*quanfa* in Chinese, *kwonbop* in Korean, *kempo* in Japanese) is taken primarily from General Qi Jiguang's manual, but mixes in a couple of illustrations from a manual on escape and seizing techniques (the possible Chinese precursor to Japanese jujutsu) with Qi's original 32 boxing forms. It is possible that a combination of Chinese boxing and seizing techniques similar to those shown in Qi's manual influenced takkyon, a nineteenth century Korean sport described as employing "flying foot" and grappling techniques (Yi, 1970: ch. 4, 479-512; No, 1974: 145). The term *takkyon* or "push the shoulders" (not taekkyon, which appears to be based on lack of knowledge of the Chinese characters or an attempt to disassociate it from possible foreign origins) infers a technique possibly similar to that used in tsuppari, paizhang, and shoupai. While takkyon is referred to as a distinctive fighting sport like subak, the term originally may have only been meant to describe a specific subak or kwonbop technique to put an opponent off balance. We are told that its association with undesirable activities such as revenge fights and gambling resulted in its prohibition and demise.

Both Koreans and Chinese had a healthy respect for the Japanese sword and Yi Dok-Mu's encyclopedia includes a section on Japanese sword techniques. Explaining that the terms for sword and knife had become intermixed, Yi presents as "native country sword" a routine using a weapon similar to the Chinese single-edged, curved broadsword (*dao* or knife in Chinese terminology) (Yi, 1970: ch. 2, 357-373).[1] Yi also associates traditional Korean sword practice with the story of Huang Chang-Rang, who is said to have been a subject of the Silla kingdom. Huang supposedly learned sword dancing at the age of seven, entered the Paekche kingdom, where crowds gathered in the city to watch him perform. His fame brought him to the attention of the Paekche king, who had him perform at court. Huang assassinated the Paekche king in the midst of his performance, was executed in Paekche and mourned as a hero in Silla and, from that time, the folk custom of performing a masked sword dance began (Yi, 1970: ch. 2, 357-373; No, 1958: ch. 21, 347).[2]

Although the references to traditional Korean martial arts are scattered and there are large gaps in information for some periods, one can see from the foregoing that it is still possible to piece together a broad outline which generally reflects Chinese influence. The Koreans appear to have modeled their military martial arts system on that prevailing as early as the Chinese Han period (206-220) and to have retained the term subak, originally associated with that period, through the fifteenth century, long after the Chinese terminology had changed. However, the term for wrestling changed from *kakjo* to *kakryuk* (Chinese, *jueli*; colloquial Korean, *sirrum*) during the Yi period (1392-1910) (Gwahakwon, 1961: 358; Yijo, 1953: juan 4, 50).

Native country (Korean) sword.

Long spear.

The historical evidence allows us to believe that traditional martial arts were part of Korean military training, and were practiced by individuals in the countryside, as late as the nineteenth century (for comparison, some traditional practices continued in the Chinese military until 1902). However, they appear to have been almost totally abandoned by the beginning of the twentieth century.

The evidence does not allow us to say, as some claim, that the traditional military skill, subak, was directly related to taekwondo or that "taekwondo is a martial art independently developed over twenty centuries ago in Korea."] However, we can say that a couple of forms called subak were practiced there over the centuries and that takkyon may have represented techniques associated with subak or kwonbop. Even modem taekkyon proponents refer to Chinese General Qi Jiguang's forms in the *Muye Dobo Tongji* in tracing their skills—this only tends to support the argument for Chinese influence (Yi, 1990). In any case, takkyon does provide a slender thread tying in "traditional" skills with the emphasis on kicks in taekwondo. Taekwondo, for the most part, though, appears to be a post-Korean War product, developed primarily from what the Koreans called *tangsudo* (karate) introduced during the period of Japanese rule.[4]

The traditional Korean martial arts are but a vague memory and tae-kwondo a symbol born in the cradle of modern Korean nationalism, a fact which should be kept in mind as we approach the 2000 Olympics in Sydney, in which taekwondo will be a featured sport.

Chinese, Korean, and Japanese References

Chonui Samguk Sagi	全譯三國史記
Dongguk Sesigi	東國歲時記
Gujin Tushu jicheng	古今圖書集成
Hanguk Cheyuksa Yongu	韓國體育史研究
Hanshu Yiwenzhi jiangshu	漢書藝文志講疏
Hwarangdo Yongu	花郎道研究
Jixiao Xinshu	紀效新書
Kokuri Hekiga Kofun to Kikajin	高句麗壁畫古墳と歸化人
Koryo Sa	高麗史
Muye Dobo Tongji	武藝圖譜通志
Nan Shi	南史
Samguk Yusa	三國遺事
Shinchong Tongguk Yoji Sungnam	新增東國輿地勝覽
Shiming	釋名
Wubei Zhi	武備志
Yijo Shillok	李朝實錄
Yijo Shillok Pullyujip	李朝實錄分類集

Chinese, Korean, and Japanese Terms

bangbakdae	防牌隊
dao	刀
hwarang	花郎
jujutsu	柔術
kakjo/juedi	角觝 角抵
kakryuk jueli/sirrum	角力
karatedo	空手道 唐手道
kwon/quan	拳
kwonbop/quanfa/kempo	拳法
paizhang	拍張
ryuksa/lishi	力士
subak/shoubo	手搏
subak/shoupai	手拍
sumo	相撲
takkyon	托肩
taekwondo	跆拳道
tangsudo/karatedo	唐手道
tode/tangshou/tangsu/karate	唐手
tsuppari	突っ張り

Individual, Dynastic, and Place Names

Former Han	前漢
Huang Chang-Rang	黃倡郎
Hwarang	花郎
King Jongjo	正祖
Koguryo	高句麗
Koryo	高麗
North Cholla	全羅北道
Paekche	百濟
Qi Jiguang	戚繼光
Sokkuram	石窟庵
South Chungchong	忠清南道
Southern & Northern Dynasties	南北朝
Tang	唐
Three Kingdoms	三國
Unified Shilla	新羅
Unjin County	恩津縣
Yi	李
Yi Dok-Mu	李德懋

Notes

[1] According to Mao Yuanyi, the Koreans also faithfully maintained traditional Chinese double-edged straight sword skills which had gone into disuse in China. In his *Encyclopedia of Military Preparedness* (*Wubei Zhi*, 1621), Mao claims "...those who are interested can find it in Korea, where the forms and techniques are fully intact. Indeed, we know it is lost in China and must be sought among the...surrounding peoples..." However, Yi pointedly questions Mao's claim, noting that, in any case, there was no evidence of this over one hundred years later.

[2] "Sword dancing" is the traditional Chinese term for sword practice, which was especially popular during the Tang, roughly contemporary with the height of the Korean Silla period.

[3] www.rpi.edu/dpt/union/taekwan/public_html/history.httml, p. 1.

[4] Use of the term *tangsudo* is surrounded by ambiguity. In Korean it means "way of Tang hands," referring to the Chinese Tang dynasty (618-960). In Japanese, the Chinese characters for *tangsudo* are pronounced *karatedo* and also mean "way of Tang hands" (or "Chinese hands"), but since the Chinese characters for both "Tang" and "empty" are pronounced *kam* in Japanese, the

term can also mean "way of the empty hand." This is now the preferred Japanese usage, although the former usage appears to have been more common when karate was first introduced to the Tokyo martial sports community from Okinawa in the 1920's (to confuse matters further, the Okinawans, who generally admit the Chinese origins of karate, originally used the *on* or so-called Chinese pronunciation of "Tang," so they pronounced karate as *tode* (long "a"). This usage distances the art from its Japanese connection and therefore would be more acceptable to Koreans, but the fact remains that taekwondo owes more to Japanese karate and less to traditional Korean martial arts than some Koreans care to admit.

References

Chen, Menglei. (1977). *Gujin tushu jicheng* (*Encyclopedia of ancient and modern literature*) *Vol. 71*. Taibei: Dingwen Shuju.

Gu, Shi. (Ed.). (1987). *Hanshu yiwenzhi jiangshu* (*Annotated Han history bibliographies*). Shanghai: Guji Chubanshe.

Gwahakwon. (1961). *Yijo Sillok Pullyujip* (*Classified index of the veritable records of the Yi Dynasty*), *Vol. 4* (*Military Matters*). Seoul: Gwahakwon.

Il Yon. (1995). *Samguk yusa* (*Memorabilia of the Three Kingdoms*) (2nd ed.). (Kim Pong-Du, Trans.). Seoul: Gyumunsa.

Kim, Un-Yong. (1978). *Taekwondo*. Seoul: Korean Overseas Information Service.

Li, Yanshou. (1936). *Nanshi* (*Southern history*). Shanghai: Zhonghua Shuju.

Liu, Xi. (1985). Shiming (Elucidation of names). In *Sikuquanshu huiyao* (*Complete library of the four treasuries*) Vol. 78, juan 3. Taibei: Taiwan Shijie Shuju.

Ministry of Foreign Affairs Republic of Korea. (1956). *Korean arts, Vol. 1 painting and sculpture*. Seoul: Ministry of Foreign Affairs Republic of Korea.

Mizuno, Masakuni. (1972). *Kokuri heikiga kofun to kikajin* (*Koguryo ancient tomb wall murals and naturalized persons*). Tokyo: Yuzan Kaku.

No, Sa-Sin. (1958). *Sinchong Dongguk yeji songnam* (*New expanded Dongguk gazetteer*). Seoul: Dongguk Munhaksa.

No, Sun-Song. (1974). *Hanguk cheyuksa yongu* (*Korean physical culture history research*). Seoul: Munsonsa.

Shin, Sa-Guk, (Ed.). (1963). *Chonui Samguk sagi* (*Complete translation of the history of the Three Kingdoms*). (Kim Chong-Kwon, Trans.). Seoul: Sonjin Munhwasa.

Yasiya Munhaksa. (1972). *Koryo sa* (*Koryo history*). Seoul: Yasiya Munhaksa.

Yi, Dok-Mu. (1970). *Muye dobo tongji* (*Encyclopedia of illustrated martial arts manuals*). Seoul: Hakmungak. Original dates from 1790.

Yi, Hyon-Gun. (1955). *Hwarangdo yongu*. Seoul: Munhwasa.

Yi, Sok-Ho. (1991). *Choson sesigi* (*Korean annual customs*). Seoul: Dong-munson.

Yi, Yong-Bok. (1990). *Hanguk muye–Taekkyon* (*The Korean martial art–Taekkyon*). Seoul: Hak Min Sa.

Yijo sillok (*Veritable records of the Yi Dynasty*). (1953). Tokyo: n.p.

chapter 2

Ancient Military Manuals and Their Relation to Modern Korean Martial Arts

Manuel E. Adrogué, LL.M.[1]

All photos courtesy of M. Adrogué, except where noted.

Introduction[2]

In the 1960s and early 1970s, when Korean martial arts first started having an impact in the Western hemisphere, many martial art students turned to books in order to obtain additional information to that provided by their teachers. Today, many of these books are considered classics. Such books were mainly "manuals," most of them available in English, as those written by Choi Hong Hi, Son Duk Song, Sihak Henry Cho, Rhin Moon Richard Chun, and Hwang Kee. Spanish speaking readers will also probably remember Lee Won II's book. Students in those days could also refer to specialized publications dealing with Korean-style forms (among the first, Jhoon Rhee's "Chon Ji" series, and Kim Pyung Soo's "Pal Gwe" series). Most of the classic manuals, as well as the majority of those written since that time, echoed and helped to foster among martial artists an acceptance of a number of historical affirmations as facts, despite their being devoid of any verifiable connection with the Korean history as described by other sources. Among the clichés used as evidence for the pretended antiquity of today's Korean martial arts were the following:

11

1) The combat fierceness and dexterity of Hwarang and Sonbae warriors.

2) The promotion in rank that the king gave to military men taking into consideration their fighting performance in championships and festivals.

3) The archeological remains illustrating guardians or "strongmen" (k., *ryuksa*; ch. *lishi*), as found in drawings, murals, and stone sculptures.

4) The successful repulse of the Japanese invaders in the 16th century.

5) The military texts that included combat training without weapons.

Nowadays, lack of interest in martial arts history is used by the industry's establishment to make up fables that only people unacquainted with Korea's historical facts can believe. On the one hand, there are leaders of technically young martial arts (Tae Kwon Do,* Tangsudo, Hapkido) who claim an antiquity for their styles of at least a thousand years; on the other hand, there are people who say that they have personally created what clearly existed before them. In other words, any person claiming that the tire is ancient and pretending to back up this assertion by showing old drawings of wheels is actually wrong, and anyone who affirms that he has invented the wheel because he has improved the tire design is giving himself credit he doesn't deserve.

> * EDITOR'S NOTE: It is the publisher's editorial policy to use "Taekwondo" as the general spelling for this art. Some people and organizations prefer using "Tae Kwon Do." Because of the author's preferences, we have used the later spelling.

Whereas historical ignorance is the rule in today's general martial arts environment, academic-related circles (spearheaded by the *Journal of Asian Martial Arts*) have made important progress. During the last five years, many authors have made some previous "ancient myths" of the martial arts bite the dust, and many interesting findings have been unearthed.

This chapter attempts to update and summarize the more recent scholars' work and their relation to individual efforts by a few of today's martial art grandmasters to rescue Korea's forgotten martial past, with emphasis on the way in which item 5 above has influenced the modern disciplines of Tae Kwon Do, Tangsudo, and Ship Pal Ki.

A SYNOPSIS OF KOREAN HISTORY

From a schematic point of view, the history of Korea can be divided into a legendary period, three classic periods, and two "modern" periods.

Pre-Historic or Legendary Period

It is believed that about 7200 B.C.E. twelve tribal groups may have founded a league called Han Kuk in the Korean peninsula and the surrounding areas. There is archeological support indicating that by 3898 B.C.E. Han Kuk consolidated as the small state of Bakdal formed by the Dong Yi ethnic group from which the Koreans, Jurchen (Manchu), Mongols, Kithans and Xiongnu (Huns) descended. In 2333 B.C.E., Dan Gun, said to be the son of the eighteenth king of Bakdal, formed the Choson dynasty.[3] Since that time, Koreans have believed that Dan Gun, mythic founder of their nation,[4] was begotten by the divine son of the solar deity, Hwan Ung, and a bear-turned-into-a-woman. These beliefs were fostered and intensified during nationalistic periods, and the Dan Gun name was used by the Korean sovereigns in the state-city of Choson who performed religious and political functions in the surroundings of Pyongyang (modern North Korea's capital city) until 194 B.C.E., when important political changes occurred.

The Three Kingdoms Period (57 B.C.E.–935 C.E.)

In addition to Choson, other "state-cities" located in the area now occupied by both Koreas and Manchuria started to organize themselves into independent realms. Koguryo (37 B.C.E.-668 C.E.), Paekche (18 B.C.E,-663 C.E.), and Silla (57 B.C.E.-935 C.E.) were the most important kingdoms, although there were other minor realms such as the Kaya league. The three principal kingdoms fought against each other, and Silla entered into an alliance with the Chinese Sui (581-618) and Tang (618-907) dynasties in order to prevail. A timely breaking of the alliance by Silla when alien forces had already occupied a great part of the territory allowed Silla's king, Moon Moo, and his warriors to succeed in expelling Chinese forces from the peninsula, which prevented the Korean people from becoming extinct by 700.[5] In those days, Buddhist doctrine had already entered into the Korean peninsula, as the monk Sundo had introduced it into the Koguryo kingdom by 372 C.E., and the monk Won Hyo had achieved its popular acceptance within Silla by 686 C.E.

Koryo Period (918–1392)

The Koryo period occurred as the unification and consolidation of Korea as a nation matured (this period gave its name to "Korea").[6] Along with the flourishing of the fine arts and the reorganization of the state, it maintained a strong military presence in view of the permanent conflict in the period between the Sung (960-1279) and the Qing (1644-1912) dynasties within neighboring China.

In 1230, after disruptions within Koryo's dynastic succession, Genghis

Khan's Mongol hordes subjugated all Asia and established the Yuan dynasty (1279-1368) in China. They dominated Koryo with extreme cruelty, including forming lines of enslaved children with ropes passing through their hands.

With respect to martial arts during this time, the Korean royal court adopted some Mongol habits, such as methods of horsemanship, archery, and wrestling. Lacking naval experience, the Mongol's drive to conquer the Japanese isles at the eastern extreme of Asia relied on Koryo's expertise. The Mongols forced Koryo to provide a military base for their plans to invade Japan in 1274 and 1281. The first invasion was initially resisted by the Japanese and was later halted due to severe climatic conditions. The second was frustrated by a typhoon which was considered by the Japanese as a "divine wind" (j. *kamikaze*). In the following decades, Koryo overcame this domination and asserted its sovereignty against the dictates of the Yuan (1279-1368) and the early Ming (1368-1644), until an internal coup ended the Koryo dynasty in 1392.

The Choson (Yi) Period (1392-1910)

An intellectual elite came to power and tried to put an end to the blemishes in the previous administration of the country by adopting Neo-Confucianism as the basic state philosophy. Such doctrine was led by an intelligentsia which esteemed intellectual effort and endeavors and despised manual labor and military affairs, trying to establish a meritocracy geared towards popular welfare. This caused contempt for the Buddhist clergy and the military men, who were deemed responsible for all the political vices of the previous years. During this period, many of Korea's Confucian scholars believed their country should culturally submit to China, the cultural center of the Eastern world.

The positioning of Korea under the cultural dictates of China coincided with the abandonment of military preparedness with the remarkable exception of King Sejong (1419-1450), a tireless genius who spread an independent and genuinely national culture among the people. Besides his fame for creating the Hangul phonetic "alphabet," King Sejong was a driving force behind the military use of gun-powder which had been extensively employed by the Chinese.[7] However, his efforts were not enough to stop the disdain of following rulers for all military matters.

In 1592, Japanese naval forces invaded Choson by surprise. The Koreans were clearly lacking in military readiness. With few resources, the Korean military and rural militias organized by monks heroically repelled the attack with some effective support from the Ming Chinese. Five years later, a second Japanese invasion found Choson duly prepared, and Korea achieved a sound victory.

Other than isolated compilations such as the *Muye Dobo Tongji*, the following centuries were times in which the military and clergymen's contribution during those war years were forgotten, and Choson sank into an imprudent decline in military preparation. Across the Eastern Sea for centuries, Japan's military steel was tempered by permanent wars between feudal lords, which shaped their society into a warrior culture. In contrast, Korea would pay a heavy price for being militarily weak during the 20th century.

During initial contacts with the West, while Japan was opened to trade with America and Europe, Korea decided to isolate itself and became known as "the hermit realm." This situation represented another disadvantage for the (then renamed) kingdom of Choson.

Japanese Occupation (1910-1945)

In 1907, the expanding Japanese Empire found a weak Korea lacking international support. Upon the basis of a fake "Protectorate Treaty," Japan occupied Korean territory and in the following years turned it into a colony. Western countries preferred to remain distant. Their sanguinary treatment of people—including tortures and abuses of the civilian population by Japanese soldiers, their insistence on the adoption of Japanese names and habits, the prohibition of the use of the vernacular language, and the expatriation of 500,000 men to work in Japan as slaves for the pre-war heavy industry—were part of an attempt to eliminate all traces of Korean culture. Such actions irremediably destroyed a great part of the past's relics. All these happened notwithstanding numerous resistance movements in international forums as well as guerilla resistance. Japan's defeat by the Allies with the atomic bombs of 1945 marked the end of this horrendous period.

Reconstruction (1945 to Today)

A few years after Korea gained its independence, the peninsula turned into the first battlefield in the international confrontation between capitalism and communism. The bloody Korean War (1950-1953) counted up to four million casualties dead and wounded, and arbitrarily divided a country that had not yet been able to find its feet. Since then, after successive military governments, the democratic system has gained some strength in South Korea during the last decade, but in North Korea a pitiless Stalinist regime still oppresses its people. Still, many South Koreans view a gradual withdrawal of U.S. military forces from their country as a precondition for the full political maturity of the divided peninsula and the achievement of unification. Not a matter to be solved easily, the threat of North Korea's nuclear power seems to call for a strong military "dissuasive" presence in the region, which the U.S. government feels obliged to provide.

IMPORTANT ANCIENT MILITARY MANUALS

With the general sketch of Korean history as presented above, we can now take a closer look at important military manuals that have had an impact on Korean martial arts as viewed today. There are some historic references that indicate that by the time of the Three Kingdoms—that is, much before General Qi's *New Books of Effective Methods* (*Ki Hyo Shin Su*)—Koreans practiced a combat form called *Subak* (k.), probably related to the Chinese *Shoubu* (ch., "hitting hand").

The Chinese *New Book of Effective Methods* and General Qi

Due to persistent raids by Japanese pirates who devastated Chinese coasts, in 1559, Chinese General Qi Jiguang (ch.; k. Chuk Kye Kwang) was appointed to put an end to the problem. He was put in command of 10,000 men and he warned them that any soldier's cowardice in battle would mean death for all his battalion. He also promised monetary rewards to every soldier bringing an enemy's head. According to British specialist Harry Cook (1998), Qi trained his men with long weapons (spears, halberds and staffs) instead of depending on projectile weapons, such as the bow and arrow or the harque-bus—the latter was less reliable because it frequently exploded in the hands of those who used it. Employing 12-man formations with special combat tactics based on the different function of each member of the group in accordance to his assigned weapon, Qi prevailed against the enemy. In the following years to meet other military challenges, Qi developed new battle tactics using war carts and different types of response to Mongol attacks coming from the north (one tactic consisted of spearmen attacking riders while other foot-soldiers annulled their mobility by cutting the horses tendons). In 1561, during his stay at the coast, General Qi wrote a troop training manual, the *New Book of Effective Methods* (ch. *Jixiao Xinshu*; k. *Ki Hyo Shin Su*). It consisted of eighteen chapters divided into six sections, including a chapter on barehanded com-bative training under the title of "Boxing Methods." The author considered that, although this type of training had little value for large-scale battle, it was nevertheless useful training for body flexibility, reflexes, hand speed, quick yet solid footwork, and jumping capacity—all of which were very valuable for a warrior. In his brief comment on combat without weapons, General Qi mentioned classic Chinese boxing methods as the Six Steps Style, Monkey Boxing, Eagle Claw, and, among the weapons he referred to, was the Shaolin staff.

Introduction of the *New Book of Effective Methods* in Korea

The first big Japanese invasion of Korea was in 1592. On April 13th, the forces of Hideyoshi Toyotomi disembarked with 200,000 men at the port of Pusan. Although the local forces were unprepared, things would have been worse if it were not for the courageous deeds of the rural people who were trained and organized by the monks Choi Hyong Ung and his disciple Sa Myong Dang.[8] After an ill-omened beginning, Korea received military support from China. The 300,000 soldiers sent by the Emperor Ming had been trained according to General Qi's *New Book of Effective Methods*, and they successfully repelled the invasion.

In 1597, Han Kyo, a governmental official considered to be an impelling force for martial arts in Korea, was put in charge of the Department of Martial Arts Training. Following a suggestion of Chinese Admiral Nak Sang Ji (k.), he prepared a course on combat technique, assisted by Chinese Master Jang Kuk Sam (k.) and ten other experts. This course trained 70 selected military men in battlefield combat technique—mainly, the use of saber, lance and multiple-headed spear—to turn them into combat instructors. Present day martial art authority and president of Korea's Ki Do Hae, In Sun Seo (1999), considers this to be the first martial arts training hall ever recorded in Korea's history.

According to highly reputed martial arts authority, Dr. Kimm He Young (May 1999), after graduation those instructors were sent to different places in the country to recruit and train soldiers. As an admission test, applicants were required to jump over a three to four foot-high fence while carrying a heavy rock. Once inducted, the recruits were trained in weaponry (including archery), running, jumping, swimming, and diving. They were also trained in sailing, strategy, and spying rudiments. These previsions, and the valuable participation of Admiral Yi Sun Shin, Korea's naval hero who defeated 133 Japanese ships with only 12 vessels,[9] caused the total frustration of the second and last invasion of Hideyoshi.

The Illustrated Martial Arts & The Book of Military Preparation

Han Kyo later wrote the *Illustrated Martial Arts* based on the Chinese *New Book of Effective Methods*. It had an added value since, for its preparation, the techniques were tested and provided with comments and illustrations. The book consisted of six sections that referred to the use of infantry combat weapons. Barehanded combat was not included, and Han Kyo stated in the introduction that the Chinese techniques of "killing hand" (k., *sal su*) and its "spinning like the wind, and progressing and retreating like lightning" could be hardly put into pictures to describe their position or methods. Han Kyo also made contact with Chinese commander Hu Yu Kyok (k.) who explained to him some aspects of "yin-yang hand" (k., *um yang su*), an aspect of martial

17

arts that included strikes, kicks and throws, and those tactics applicable to the use of weapons. It is interesting to note that modern hwarangdo founder Lee Joo Bang claims to have learned the ancient "um-yang kwon" combat skills in So Kwang Temple during the 1940's from monk Suahm Dosa, reportedly a lineage holder of the hwarang warrior tradition.

In China, during the first half of the 17th century, Mao Yuanyi (k., Mo Won Ui) wrote the *Book of Military Preparation* (k. *Mubiji*; j., *Bubiji*) with 240 chapters. Contemporary authors disagree with respect to the publication date. Harry Cook (1999) and Patrick McCarthy (1996) state that it was published in 1621 whereas, according to Kimm He Young, it was published in 1644. Cook states that even though they share the same name, this is not the *Book of Military Preparation* known in Okinawa and very much appreciated by later karate greats, Miyagi Chojun, Funakoshi Gichin and Mabuni Kenwa. The Okinawan *Book of Military Preparation* is considered to be derived from a work written in China's Fujian Province based on the Yongchun village White Crane boxing style (according to Kinjo Akio, the place and system where Seisan karate kata originated), and does not include the use of weapons but describes techniques, vital points, herbal medicine and tactics (Yang, 1993). So, whereas the *Book of Military Preparation* written by Mo was a military manual (an essential precedent to the *Muye Dobo Tongji*), another book became known under the same name in Okinawa which was strictly on southern Chinese boxing. It is interesting to note that (i) both versions are of Chinese origin, and (ii) the version spread in Okinawa, in this author's opinion, has been more influential on Korea's modern Tae Kwon Do and Tangsudo than the Korean-adopted version (despite grandmaster Hwang Kee's efforts).

Mo's version included information on the *bon kuk kom* (original national saber, from Silla), a weapon that became famous due to Kwan Chang Rang, son of Silla Hwarang General Pum Il, whose attempt to murder the Paekche king ended with his life in the 7th century. Kwan Chang Rang was famous for his ability with the saber and the enemy's king demanded a demonstration. During the demonstration, Kwan thrusted his blade into the monarch's chest with a swift and unexpected movement. Silla warriors organized a saber routine in his memory in which the player wears a mask to represent the sacrificed young man. This tradition has been kept alive in Korea's rural festivals until today.[10] In this way the tradition of this saber is preserved, whose remote origins are to be found in China, according to Yi Dok Mu (k., also Lee Dok Moo), and it might be the predecessor of the famed Japanese sword.

The Silla saber technique's effectiveness and the sober elegance of it in motion, devoid of any superficialities, attest that its preservation for many centuries was not simply due to the region's folklore, but it was considered a valuable defensive weapon. The inclusion of the Korean saber in a Chinese manual would reveal the importance that it had gained in the region in the old days. When analyzing the saber technique by its description in the referred manuals, Della Pia (1995) asserts that although some Chinese influence can be perceived, there is a strong case for the origin of the weapon and its techniques in the Korean peninsula.

Toward the end of the 17th century, King Suk Jong gave impetus to the re-establishment of combat arts by organizing festivals that included wrestling and archery competitions (mounted and on foot) and by forming a special group of elite warriors called the *Byul Kun Jik* in 1694. He appointed Kim Che Gun as part of a diplomatic mission to Japan. Kim eventually received instruction in the local saber techniques and he remained abroad until he had learned four saber styles. His acquired knowledge was reportedly transmitted orally until its incorporation into the *Muye Dobo Tongji* a century later.

The *Muye Shinbo*, *Muye Dobo Tongji*, and the Eighteen and Twenty-Four Military Techniques

In 1756, on behalf of King Yung Jo, Prince Regent Se Ju Sa Do ordered the preparation of *Muye Shinbo*, a manual based on the *Muye Jebo* but that included twelve additional weapons and techniques. It took three years to prepare this book, which included eighteen sections in total. Due to the way the prince referred to it, this military manual became famous as the *Bon Jo Muye Ship Pal Ban* (k., "The Eighteen Martial Art Categories of the Yi Dynasty"). People who had some formal instruction in martial arts were reputed as knowledgeable in the "Eighteen Techniques" (k., *Ship pal ki*, *Ship pal ban*, or *Ship pal jon*).

In 1789, King Jeongjo requested the preparation of a new military manual because differences in technique and concept among the officers made it difficult to teach the troops using the *Muye Shinbo*. Unlike the previous books, which were mainly referential, it has been said that this manual was meant to be a practical guide to all military technique, and should encompass everything known about training warriors at the time. In the foreword, King Jeongjo stated that:

> Through diligently practicing these methods and mastering the strategy of the dragon and the tiger, the soldiers protecting the capital and the talented military officers will become agile warriors and loyal soldiers who will not abandon their country. My true intention of publishing this expanded volume of military tactics is to record this instruction for posterity.

Yi Dok Mu, considered its main author, assumed the task of gathering, comparing and commenting on the bibliographical background. Park Je Ga was in charge of the manual's structure, and Park Dong Su's responsibility was the testing of the techniques. The result, called the *Muye Dobo Tongji* (k., *Complete Illustrated Martial Arts Manual*) was published in 1790. It took as its principal basis the *Mubiji* and the *Muye Shinbo*, and it added six new sections, all referring to weapons to be used on horseback, probably related to the Mongol experience. The new manual was much more than a simple digest. It was a recollection of most of the military precedents in the Far East, and its thoughtful comments made this an extraordinary work. Although contemporary martial art experts, Hwang Kee and Kimm He Young, had done research and produced publications on the *Muye Dobo Tongji's* "boxing" chapter, trying to interpret its arcane content (the former, by the 1960s, and the latter, in the 1990s), it was not until 2000 that Tae Kwon Do authority Sang H. Kim published a complete translation from the ancient Chinese used in Korea into the English language, thus making its knowledge available to the world's English speaking enthusiasts.

The manual is divided into four volumes and includes 24 training sections: six sword methods, one sword training system, one shield and blade method, nine long battle weapons, five weapons to be used by riders as well as a ball game on horseback, and a boxing section. Each section illustrates a practice routine that depicts the ways to use each weapon. With slight variations, each section has the following structure:

a) Weapon illustration—including the Chinese, Korean, and Japanese version as the case may be.

b) The explanations originally given by General Qi and Master Han Kyo with comments on the subject from Mo's work and historical or practical references by Yi Dok Mu.

c) Illustrated description of the routine with technical instructions for solo execution. It should be noted that sometimes it is difficult to follow the instructions on how to get from one position to another, because there are no illustrations of the transitions.

d) Diagrams of each routine, with its movements indicated by their names.

e) Diagrams of movements using human figures. For the Japanese saber, a section with combat applications is also included.

We emphasize that, traditionally, archery had been a highly developed warrior activity ("the national art of Korea," according to the introduction of the *Muye Dobo Tongji*, which reminds us of the saying, "the saber in Japan, the bow in Korea, and the spear in China"). However, this weapon was not included in the books mentioned in this chapter. This can be related to General Qi's idea of giving more importance to close-quarters combat training, and it is also a hint that strengthens the hypothesis that these manuals were based on Chinese models. Such circumstance leads us to conclude that these manuals do not include all the combat techniques of the time, since they only include those that were considered useful for training military men in large formations for mass warfare.

A-1) "Ambushing Posture" (*mae bok seh*) described and illustrated in the *Muye Dobo Tongji*. **A-2)** Hwang Kee adopts this posture while performing Hwa Son hyung. *Photo from Hwang, K. (1992).* **A-3)** Author showing the same posture in the way recreated by Kimm He Young interpreting the *Muye Dobo Tongji's* instructions and drawings.

B-1 & 2) "Double-handed defense"—a characteristic hard style movement found in modern Tae Kwon Do and karate. It is a technique that resembles the old "seven star fist posture" of the *Muye Dobo Tongji* (refer to original drawing). There is controversy on whether it was originally a block or a fist strike.

The following chart, based on Sang H. Kim's works, enumerates the training specialties included in the above-mentioned military manuals using the order provided by the *Muye Dobo Tongji*:

MUYE JEBO (6)	MUYE SHINBO ("Ship pal ki") (18)	MUYE DOBO TONG JI Vol. (24)	DESCRIPTION
Jang Chang	Jang Chang	I. 1. Jang Chang	**Spear** About 5', flexible wood, used during the recovery of Pyong Yang in January 1593.
------------	Juk Jang Chang	2. Juk Jang Chang	**Long Bamboo Spear** About 20', flexible.
------------	Ki Chang	3. Ki Chang	**Flag Spear** About 9'2"blade; the flag and its fast changes made it a deceptive weapon.
Dang Pa	Dang Pa	4. Ki Chang	**Triple-bladed spear** Trident, 7'6"to 18'; defensive usage.
------------	------------	5. Ma Sang Ki Chang	**Spear on Horseback** About 15'; used to charge against enemy.
Nang Son	Nang Son	II. 6. Nang Son	**Wolf Spear** About 15', iron or flexible wood, used to dismount riders.
Ssang Su Do	Ssang Su Do	7. Ssang Su Do (Jang do; Yong Kom; Pyong Kom)	**Two-handed Curved Saber** About 6'5"; powerful, maybe originated in the Japanese fora tachi of earlier centuries and then adopted by Koreans and Chinese.
------------	Ye Do	8. Ye Do (Dan Do; Hwan Do)	**Short Saber** about 4'4"; originally from China, it was preserved in Korea and Japan.
------------	Wae Kom	9. Wae Kom	**Foreign Sword (Japanese)** The reputation of the Japanese saber determined its inclusion circa 17th century.
------------	Kyo Jon	10. Kyo Jon	**Partner Sword Training** Kim (2000) mentions that, according to Japanese manuals, it was to be used for double-edged swords; in Korea it was adapted for single-edged sabers.
------------	Ssang Kom	III. 11. Je Do Kom	**Admiral's Straight Sword** Developed and successfully used by Yi Yu Song, based on spinning when surrounded by many enemies.

-----------	Bon Kuk Kom	12. Bon Kuk Kom	**Original National Saber (from Shilla)** Ancient technique used by Korea's Hwarang.
-----------	Ssang Kom	13. Ssang Kom	**Twin Swords** About 4'4"; used alternating for attack and defense.
-----------	-----------	14. Ma Sang Ssang Kom	**Twin Swords on Horseback** They were usually short, but the legendary Ji An fought with a 7' saber in each hand.
-----------	Wol Do	15. Wol Do	**Moon / Crescent Sword (Halberd)** Mostly considered a training weapon.
-----------	-----------	16. Ma Sang Wol Do	**Halberd on Horseback** Used during the Japanese invasions.
-----------	Hyop Do	17. Hyop Do	**Narrow Bladed Spear-Sword** Similar to the Japanese naginata, it was rarely used in battle as it was not considered strong enough.
Dong Pae	Dong Pae	18. Dong Pae	**Shield** Rattan or branch woven, sometimes covered with leather. It was used with the ye do sword or the articulated staff to fend off throwing weapons; widely used in China (*t'eng pai*); in Okinawa (*tin be*) it was made up of turtle shields.
-----------	Kwon Bop	IV. 19. Kwon Bop	**Fist Method** Chinese origin.
Kon Bang	Kon Bang	20. Kon Bang Chang	**Long Staff** 7' long; it sometimes had a 2" blade on one tip; used to thrust and strike, it was considered the basic weapon.
-----------	Pyon Kon	21. Pyon Kon	**Whip-Staff** Articulated, a long section of 8' was linked by chain to a shorter 2' section. It was used to defend fortresses against climbers.
-----------	-----------	22. Ma Sang Pyon Kon	**Whip-Staff on Horseback** The chain was longer, and the short section used to have iron nails.
-----------	-----------	23. Ma Sang Kyok Ku	**Competitive Sport Riding** Riding training in a competitive sport similar to polo which was appreciated as a spectator sport by the court.
-----------		24. Ma Sang Jae	**Equestrian Acrobacy** Riding skills that included hiding at the horse's side, standing atop, or pretending to be dead.

Nowadays, the teaching curriculum of the *Muye Dobo Tongji* is preserved by the Korean Kyongdang education organization based in Kwang Ju, South Korea and lead by folk martial arts expert Lim Dong Kyu. This organization aims to educate the youth using the physical, and intellectual military standards of the Choson Dynasty. It teaches the *Muye Eeshipsa Ban* consisting of 1204 techniques in the 24 specialties, including a sword with a length of 53" (1.35 meters) that weighs 5.5 pounds (2.5 kilograms) and lances that vary from 6.5 to 19 feet in length (2 to 6 meters).

Left: Han Mu Do founder and martial arts scholar, Kimm He Young, poses with master Lim Dong Kyu. Master Lim is the foremost authority and teacher on the ancient Korean twenty-four warrior techniques. *Photo courtesy of Kimm He Young.* Right: Sang H. Kim, renowned authority in the Korean styles and hand-to-hand combat, translated the *Muye Dobo Tongji.* Here he executes a round knee kick (*murup chaki*). *Photo courtesy of Turtle Press.*

The "Boxing Section" and Modern Interpretations

The task of translating the *Muye Dobo Tongji* represented ten years of work for Sang H. Kim, a Tae Kwon Do, Hapkido and Junsado master who lives in Connecticut. As an authority in martial arts training, Kim admits that the book does not have enough details to precisely reproduce the forms that it contains.

In the boxing section (which bears the same "Kwon Bop" title as its forerunners), the manual provides names and some background information about older martial arts teaching. Among others, it states that fist art training is based on pre-established patterns (k., *hyung*), but it should be applied disregarding them. There are also tales about a Wudang Daoist master's prowess, and the superiority of internal over external styles. After mentioning that there were eighteen types of footwork, Yi Dok Mu points out that there was a system organized into six patterns (k., *yuk ro*) and ten levels (k., *ship dan kum*).

In the introductory part, the manual describes the performance of numerous techniques. According to one of them: "*Du Mun* is performed by lowering the left shoulder and fist and punching upward while the right hand pushes out horizontally to the front and bends outwards." After many similar instructions, the author concludes that: "the *yuk ro* is similar to *ship dan kum*. In general, *yuk ro* methods are used to develop bone strength in order to inflict immediate damage in a combat emergency, whereas the *ship dan kum* is for inducing a delayed reaction."[11]

After other instructions of a similar nature, the authors state that extreme emphasis in teaching a specific technique to overcome another (such as those found in the Okinawan *Bubishi*, "phoenix spreads its wings wins against dragon spits pearls," explained as "if a person throws a short punch at you, trap the attack and gouge his eyes") had taken all naturalness from practice, depriving it from its own essence, and turning those actions into nothing more than a game. When looking at the commented illustrations, the modern martial arts scholar will find some familiar positions such as "seven stars fist posture" (*chil song kwon se*, similar to "supporting block," *momtong koduro bakkat mak ki*), "single whip posture" (*yodan pyon se*, similar to "vertical ascending punch," *pande ollio sewo jirugi*), "crouching tiger posture" (*bok ho se*, similar to "mountain leaning side block," *palmok santul makki*), "high block posture" (*dang du pose*, similar to "pushing concentration block," *balwi mil ki*) and "ambushing posture" (*mae bok se*, a low and stretched position).

I should emphasize that these and many other positions have not reached the 20th century martial arts as a result of master-to-student transmission throughout generations, but modern organizations have included them in their forms, maybe sometimes even imitating ancient illustrations and thus "reviving them," trying in this way to gain an ancestral pedigree disguising the fact that modern Tae Kwon Do has no direct relation with the *Muye Dobo Tongji*. The aforementioned techniques are superficially similar to the original, but their purpose seems to be different. The illustrated routines (k., *hyung*) in the manual are very skimpy in the use of kicks, mostly limited to a few mid-height front and fan (crescent) kicks, and the fist techniques are not similar or related to any modern Korean martial art style. The "genealogical" relation of the techniques shown in the manual with those currently practiced in Tae Kwon Do or Tangsudo seems to be, to a large extent, a product of wishful thinking.

Martial art manuals reveal different "trends" of the Chinese boxing systems that arrived to Korea. In the *Muye Dobo Tongji*, we can find the inward crescent kick, directed to the rival's solar plexus, which is practiced hitting against the kicker's opposing palm (k., *an pyojok chaki*, found in today's Han Soo, Yoo Sin and Ul Ji Tae Kwon Do forms). This kick, of gymnastic value but questionable combat effectiveness, is very frequent in Shaolin styles, and was introduced to Okinawa karate from southern China. During the early 20th century, this kicking technique voyaged from Okinawa to Japan through *Ro hai* (j.) / *No pae* (k.) and *Sei san* (j.) / *Ship sam* (k.) (or j. *Han getsu* / k. *Ban wol*) routines, and from there to Korea, where it is currently performed at head-height. In other words, the presence of this technique in today's Tae Kwon Do is not a result of genuine Korean ancestry; it comes from China in an odyssey which, as a relevant milestone, in most cases includes the Shotokan karate as practiced by Funakoshi (Gigo) Yoshitaka around 1940, the Japanese style upon which the great majority of the present formal "Korean" forms were built (Cook, 2001). While Chung Do Kwan, Moo Duk Kwan, Song Moo Kwan and Oh Do Kwan were influenced by Shotokan, Chang Moo Kwan was based on Toyama's Shudokan, and Ji Do Kwan's post-1950 technique was built on Yoon Kwe Byung's Shito-ryu training. The softer and more flowing Chinese and indigenous Taekyon systems, although frequently credited as sources for Tae Kwon Do, did not provide any material technical influence on modern Tae Kwon Do and Tangsudo forms.

The recently deceased Grandmaster Hwang Kee, the founder of Moo Duk Kwan and pioneer of Tang Soo Do (who refused to use the Tae Kwon Do name), admitted that when he found the *Muye Dobo Tongji* in the National Library of Seoul in 1957, a whole new world within the martial arts opened for him. The impact of this discovery was so strong that he decided to change the name of his Tangsudo martial art into "Soo Bahk Do" because the Subak appellative is used in the manual's boxing section as the name of a barehanded combat style. Hwang Kee was truly the first internationally renowned Korean martial arts exponent who paid serious attention to the *Muye Dobo Tongji*.

During the years following his discovery, Hwang Kee studied the Kwon Bop section and revived (as far as it was possible) a series of six routines called *Yuk Ro* and another series of ten routines called *Ship Dan Gum*, apart from the *Hwa Son* (k.) routine, which he officially presented in November 1982. The Yuk Ro techniques include forward stances ("bow and arrow," according to the Chinese tradition) with circular simultaneous strikes to the front and back in a windmill action, horizontally as well as vertically, and sudden direction variations and weight shifts, pushes to the front with the palms and open-handed parrying movements. Master Hwang Hyun Chul, son of Hwang Kee and world-class technical authority in his own right, describes the routines recreated by his father from the *Muye Dobo Tongji* as a combination of hard and soft movements of profound content.

The resemblance of many movements within these (presumed Korean) forms to northern China's Long Boxing (ch. *Changquan*; k. *Jang Kwon*), which is considered the ancient predecessor of Shaolin, is remarkable. In addition, it should be noted that Hwang Kee included in his school curriculum a series of seven routines which he created called *Chil Song* (k.), generally translated as "seven stars," or more precisely, "the seventh star," [12] probably taken from the Chinese martial arts teaching that he learned during his stay in Manchuria.

Jumping Descending Fist Attack (*twimyo neryo chon kwon jiruki*)—a typical Moo Duk Kwan fighting stratagem that combines the agility, aggressiveness, and unpredictability of Korean styles with the linear fist techniques cultivated in Japanese karate. A high crescent kick (*sandan an pyojok chaki*), found in the ancient Korean martial art records and included in forms of modern Tae Kwon Do, Tangsudo, karate and Shaolin-derived styles.

Some critics doubt that Hwang Kee was ever in a position to learn a true Chinese style when, after 1931, Manchuria was a puppet state with the Japanese name of Manchukuo. However, Hwang Kee never hid the fact that he had studied a book on Japanese karate during the late 1930s and provided information to verify his Chinese martial art training. In this connection, he revealed his Manchurian master's name (k. Yang Kuk Jin), and stated that he learned "steps method" (k. *seh bop*; ch. *pu fa*), "discipline method" (k., *ryon bop*, hardening), "twelve steps of spring leg" (k. *dham toi ship ee ro*, ch. *tam tuei*, a basic Long Boxing form), and some *tae kuk kwon* (k.; ch., *taijiquan*). It is difficult to determine how many of these Chinese practices influenced Tang-sudo except for the circular and wide trajectories of the karate techniques he redesigned, and the heel-against-the-floor/toes-up mantis sweeping technique which Hwang preferred to the more popular Japanese *ashi-barai* sole sweeping style found in standard Tae Kwon Do (adopted, for instance, by General Choi in the Tae Kwon Do *Sam Il* and *Moon Moo* routines).

Furthermore, Hwang Kee's inclusion of material from the *Muye Dobo Tongji* was overshadowed by Moo Duk Kwan/ Tangsudo's precocious reputation as an effective combination of Japanese karate with Korean kicking skills. When Hwang Kee introduced techniques from the *Muye Dobo Tongji* (and the information contained within them) to the style, Moo Duk Kwan had already made a name for itself and an important number of instructors had left the original (Tang Soo Do) nucleus, in many cases joining Tae Kwon Do groups. Hence, such additions did not reach or attract the majority of those practicing the Moo Duk Kwan style. In other words, these forms arrived too late to have substantial influence over the style's already mature character. In any case, there is no doubt that Professor Hwang Kee must be credited as a precursor in the study of the *Muye Dobo Tongji*. The culmination of this effort was realized in his development of contemporary Soo Bahk Do Moo Duk Kwan.

Hwang Hyun Chul performs a two-direction fist technique
from a *Muye Dobo Tongji* derived hyung. Notice its resemblance
to Chinese Long Fist. *Photo courtesy of Hwang Hyun Chul.*

In 1999, Dr. Kimm He Young presented to the martial arts media his recreation of the illustrations and explanations of the book, the *Kwon Bop Bu Hyung* (k.), consisting of 42 complex movements. According to Kimm, the first 28 movements are for solo practice and from number 29 on, a training partner is needed and the form is performed by two men, similar to practice methods used in Chinese styles and, their imitation, in Doshin So's Japanese Shorinji Kempo (j.). Henning (2000), a precise and thoughtful author, asserts that the *Muye Dobo Tongji* illustrations are based on those of General Qi, except for the escape and seizing techniques, which might be either original, or more probably, derived from other sources, such as another Chinese manual. Dr. Kimm's movements lack the sudden focus (muscular contraction and snap action) found in Tangsudo and Tae Kwon Do, and his form does not include postures which have become common in modern karate-related martial arts, even though there are some techniques that can be recognized (front kick, inward crescent open palm kick, side mountain block, and various fist strikes). In this author's personal opinion, the way Dr. Kimm performs his routine seems to be very close to the original, since his personal background in Korean "softer" styles (Kuk Sool, Hapkido, Yudo) has prevented him from introducing more recent Japanese karate-like (abrupt) kinetic characteristics in his reconstruction of the old forms.

As we have already stated, the ample forward and backward strikes shown in the *Muye Dobo Tongji* illustrations seem to follow the Chinese Long Fist technical guidelines. In respect to the characteristic of simultaneous multidirectional actions for which Long Fist is known, Adam Hsu (n.d.) comments:

> No, it is not an exotic training in which the apprentice learns to knock two rivals at the same time, one smaller in the front and the taller by the rear. This is mental training and can be found in all the movements of the Long Fist forms... The tunnel vision is a variation of the single direction approach, overly exclusive and restricted. The apprentice's attention is reduced even more to a specific area such as the rival's fist that approaches him or to his own leg prepared to attack. However, when somebody hits with his foot in Long Fist, he must keep one arm ahead and the other arm behind in the exact position... As the apprentice moves to superior levels and starts to feel the movement as part of his body, he must learn to direct his attention to the torso, pelvis and legs.

According to Hsu, by the time the student reaches a higher level, the wide and complex movements of Long Fist shall have given him "the ability to concentrate on his rival and, simultaneously, to be alert of his surroundings with a powerful multidirectional conscience."

These benefits, as well as the special capacity that the movements of Long Boxing have for preparing the apprentice for the use of weapons, may have recommended it to General Qi and Master Han Kyo as training for the military.

About The Eighteen Techniques (*Ship Pal Ki*)

It is noteworthy that in Hwang Kee's *Soo Bahk Do Dae Kam* manual (1978) there are two different lists of eighteen techniques. They are both described as "Ship Pal Ki" and neither coincides with the list of the *Muye Shinbo*. Even though one of Hwang's lists does show some similarity to the latter—such as, different types of lances and sabers for battle—in the descriptions by Hwang there are weapons such as the bow, crossbow, and whip. Any attempt to fully analyze such lists is very difficult, as in Hwang Kee's book they are in Chinese ideograms only, and many of such characters refer to old weapons that are no longer in use. We have identified only a few of them and we have not been able to find their meaning in Chinese-Korean dictionaries.

An additional series of Eighteen Techniques, also different from those listed in the *Muye Shin Bo*, has survived to our time. It is the series taught by Yoo Sam Nam, a Ship Pal Ki (which he has romanized as "Sipalki") martial art master who has lived and taught in Argentina for more than thirty years (Yoo, n.d.). Yoo includes the following specialties in his teaching:

1. *Ho Sin Sul*: Self-defense
2. *Kyo Yon*: Pugilism, one against many
3. *Kwob Bop*: Pugilism, one against one
4. *Nang Kon*: Articulated sticks (short and symmetrical) also called *ssang jol kon* (c., *nung cha kung*; j., *nunchaku*)
5. *Dan Bong*: Short stick
6. *Bong*: Long staff, also called *jang bong*
7. *Kom*: Saber
8. *Dan Kom*: Short sword (knife)
9. *Ssang Kom*: Double sword (knives)
10. *Chung Ion Do*: Sword (*ion do* means "dragon sword," a name used in ancient China)
11. *Bang Pe*: Shield
12. *Ssan*: Belt/sash
13. *Pyon Sul*: Whip
14. *Chang*: Spear
15. *Chong Kom*: Bayonet (j., *ju ken*, literally "long saber")
16. *Jwan*: Brass knuckle
17. *Doki*: Axe
18. *Kung Sul*: Archery

Ship Pal Ki sequence by Park Joon Hyun and Portalea in 1980. C-1) Guard stance. C-2) Attack with roundhouse kick (*dollyo chaki*). C-3) Jam, trap, and secure the kicking leg. C-4) Counterattack with a low cross kick to genitals. *Photos courtesy of Miguel Hladilo and Yudo Karate magazine.*

Ship Pal Ki sequence by Park Joon Hyun and Portalea in 1980. D-1) Guard stance with staff. D-2) Direct staff attack, and sidestepping check defense. D-3) Progression in defensive maneuver cross stance (*kyo cha ja seh*). D-4) Back-knuckle counterstrike (*yi-kwon chiki*). *Photos courtesy of Miguel Hladilo and Yudo Karate magazine.*

31

What are the reasons behind the difference between Hwang Kee's and Yoo Soo Nam's lists and those of the *Muye Shinbo* digest? We must take into account that in Korea, after the publication of the *Muye Dobo Tongji* in 1790, large scale battles against mounted invaders had lost importance as probable combat scenarios (Henning, 2000, states that many sections of the *Muye Dobo Tongji* had already lost all practical value by the time of its publication). Following the success of the campaigns against the Japanese invasions, and after that danger had been overcome, a decline and abandonment of military training was the norm in Korea, even though many former soldiers continued practicing martial arts within their families. Logically, most techniques designed to face mounted enemies were replaced by infantry weapons, techniques, and martial arts training concentrated on these things.

Battlefield combat training gave way to personal combat training, and other weapons became more important (i.e., short stick, double short stick, articulated sticks). Likewise, according to Suh In Hyuk, many Korean improvised arms—as the cane, rope, or fan—were developed or improved by the court's guards due to their need for effective combatives in places where no weapons were allowed. In 1958, after decades spent learning from his family and many other instructors, Grandmaster Suh In Hyuk, whose grandfather, Suh Myong Duk, had been a Royal Court instructor, organized the arts of the Kuk Sool Won (k., "National Techniques Academy") to preserve the Korean national martial culture that existed before the 20th century Japanese occupation. His approach was intended to rescue the Court's martial arts, Buddhist martial arts (which he went to temples to learn), and the folk martial arts (as the paradigmatic case of Yoo's family). Kuk Sool has movements and weapons whose continuity, circularity, and positions show an important Chinese influence.

We should note that other "small" or "personal" weapons (such as those used by bodyguards, policemen or martial artists outside the army), which were historically used in southern China, the Ryukyu archipelago, and Indochina, were also used in Korea. The available evidence credits China as their most likely origin, but it is not a clear matter. Those weapons include the articulated sticks (j. *nunchaku*), the side handled truncheon (j. *tonfa*) and the short trident (j. *sai*). In Okinawa, due to the prohibition of weapons production, police and palace guards imported those weapons from Fuzhou. Even nowadays many people wrongly believe that the efficient Chinese personal weapons are rural Okinawa tools, but this is true only for a few of them, such as the sickle and the oar.

In Korea, miliary activity stagnated in the isolation and emphasis of Confucianism during the 18th and 19th centuries. However, families in some villages preserved the old combat techniques. At the beginning of the 20th century, they were polished by those who knew them in order to transmit these fighting skills to their sons to protect themselves against Japanese oppression. This explains situations such as the Yoo family's (holders of the *Ion Bi Ryu* "flying swallow branch") Ship Pal Ki family tradition, that kept a core of centuries-old knowledge and its name (Ship Pal), and somehow managed to keep the number eighteen while including modern weapons (such as the bayonet) and discarding those that had become outdated.

Another beneficiary of the Ship Pal Ki martial legacy is Professor He Young Kimm, who learned Ship Pal Ki from his master, Kim Swang Sub, and Professor Baek Wu Hyon, chief instructor of Jun Mu Kwan of the Korean Association of Ship Pal Ki. The Eighteen Techniques taught in this Association are not described in this chapter.[13]

During the 19th century, these Ship Pal Ki techniques, originally developed for training troops in the use of weapons, maintained combat effectiveness as they were transformed into "familiar" arts, but were not absorbed by bare-handed martial arts of Taekkyon or Subak, both which have been depicted as distinct, weaponless, combat disciplines. Taekkyon mostly converted into a popular athletic kicking and tripping folk game which has survived until our days (Ouyang, 1997). Subak is a reportedly lost combat art that had turned into military sport before fading away during the Choson period. Such distinctions are elaborations of often repeated information lacking verifiable sources and therefore remain questionable. Although the Ship Pal Ki (weapons-dominated) trend is not known to have mixed with these hand and foot fighting systems, it is probable that any Korean soldier with knowledge of both trends would have merged them.

Yon Bi Ryu Sipalki Grandmaster Yoo Soo Nam from Buenos Aires,
Argentina, showing a pressure point on an attacker's arm.

33

To understand the probable way Ship Pal Ki combat training evolved to the present time, we should consider the training received by modern members of the special forces (Cremona, personal interview, November 2001). They practice shooting with long weapons; physical conditioning; swimming; diving; close-quarter bare-hand and bladed weapons combat; explosives instruction; indoor combat tactics; urban and open field (including forest and jungle) tactics; rappel training; parachute basics, etc. This relates the fundamental ideas behind ancient Ship Pal Ki to survival of a certain family group, according to its leading authority in Argentina. Ship Pal Ki included a series of different combative skills—mostly related to weapons —that set this discipline apart from the more popular naked-hand combat arts. Ship Pal Ki techniques never became "overspecialized" in any single ability, in the same way that special forces members are not extraordinary swimmers, champion marksmen, or accomplished martial artists, but are highly functional in each area to make up extraordinary human weapons. This martial art continued its evolution keeping the ability to deal with life or death situations at the core.

Staffs and swords are out of place in modern society, and the increasing lack of reality in their practice (which was Ship Pal Ki's original goal) may have caused Master Yoo's Ship Pal Ki school to concentrate on practicing bare-handed combat skills. Among its features are a peculiar strategy of surprise and fierceness, a wide-range of technical resources (circular hand motions and footwork unusual for karate-derived traditions), the extensive use of grabbing while striking, an emphasis on combat against multiple opponents, and the use of the fingers to hit sensitive areas with rapid movements. These make up the arsenal of this Korean style as taught in Argentina (Yoo, n.d.).

During the last thirty years, the Yoo Soo Nam Ship Pal Ki system has also incorporated kicking techniques found in other Korean systems, enlarging and giving more detail to the weaponless one-on-one combat practice (without losing the weapons techniques), thus trying to preserve the effectiveness and original *raison d'être* of this martial art.

Epilogue

Research for this chapter was conducted in the hope of finding a realistic explanation connecting historical development to the technique of Korean martial arts as they are performed today. From an historical perspective, it becomes apparent that any appeal to the *Muye Dobo Tongji* as evidence for the antiquity of any Korean modern art is unacceptable today. The nationalistic arguments that have so frequently distorted the historical truth can no longer be accepted.

It is clear that, in the past, national borders had little importance if any in the development of martial arts of the Far East. Although the concept of "style" is not new in combative training, the idea of different "martial arts" as separate activities networking with affiliated instructors and followers all-around the world is indeed a novelty which has both positive consequences (i.e., access to organized knowledge which might otherwise be difficult; standardized curriculum, etc.) and negative side effects (i.e., excessive focus on the style's identity and its methods, unawareness of alternative ways used by other systems to solve the same problems).

The larger the group, the less frequently the head of a martial art system will be able to train and personally instruct a significant proportion of his students. In these cases, there is a tendency for such a system to have fewer changes than one in which the group is closely bound. As in the first case, the style will probably have difficulties going beyond the understanding of the essential concepts that give distinct identity to that style. The smaller the group, the more rapidly changes will be introduced. A clear example is Bruce Lee's backyard style which evolved at incredible speed.

A Tae Kwon Do jumping twist kick (*timyo bit-uro chaki*) developed
on the basis of Taekkyon's *jae cha ki* (which strikes with the instep),
but uses the metatarsal area of the sole for concentrated impact.

Another feature to be taken into account is the focus of the technical central authority of the style, and the (distant) instructor's priorities. In widespread styles, it is frequent to see important divergences between the ideas supporting a style and the mindset of some of its instructors (Is the style, as taught by the central authorities, geared towards keeping a tradition? Is it about cultivating a sport? Is it mainly for self-defense? How do these categories relate to the proposed style, and to the way classes are taught? Are the students conscious of what they are getting, or do they have a distorted or fantastic image?)

The ancients had no trouble in accepting foreign teachings when their security depended on it. When doing so, they were careful to learn from specialists in those martial arts—a wise and humble attitude, unlike the common behavior of intending to gain knowledge from other martial art systems by the do-it-yourself "copy-and-paste" system. On the other hand, as survival seems not to be an issue in most present-day martial arts, many profitable pseudo martial arts "corporations" have developed on the basis of convincing speeches and dubious techniques. The very basics of bare-handed training according to the Korean manuals—to boost courage in the battlefield by providing the soldiers with strong, agile and well-balanced bodies—seems to be fading away. Each instructor is responsible for what he teaches to his students, and he must decide whether to follow Master Han Kyo's example of making an effort to study in order to give his troops the best training available, or to abrogate that responsibility to a "federation" headquartered many miles away, whose interests may be other than the authenticity and combat value of what is taught in class.

If we learn from history, the past will prove useful for our lives. If we as martial art instructors make the right decisions, it will be our technical and moral contribution to this Oriental martial art legacy. In other words, our work as instructors, if only to a small extent (but noticeable to our students), will have improved the world we live in.

Acknowledgment
In gratitude to my teacher Pedro Florindo, his instructors masters Lee Chong Seo (Moo Duk Kwan) and Yang Dae Chol (Ji Do Kwan), and those preceding them. If not for their commitment to the martial Way, I would have not received such a wonderful gift, which I get to open, enjoy, and share every day. I also want to thank my right-hand man instructor Leo Di Lecce and my other students, specially the Discioscias (father and son) and Diego Cruz.

Notes

1 Regarding terminology used in this chapter, "k." stands for Korean; "j." for Japanese; and "ch." for Chinese terms. Other than certain terms referring to weapons used in southern China, for which their Cantonese name is shown with a "c.", all Chinese terms are Mandarin. Korean and Japanese terms are written without following any standard romanization system, as they have been available from different sources derived from their phonetic version. Okinawan weapon names are referred by their widely-known Hogen dialect, labeled as Japanese.

2 This work has been largely based on the illuminating studies on the ancient Chinese and Korean manuals and related subjects authored by Kimm (1999), Kim S.H. (2000), Young (1993), Henning (2000), Della Pia (1994, 1995), Pieter (1994), Cook (1998, 1999, 2001), and McCarthy (1996).

3 This kingdom is nowadays called "Ko" (old) Choson, as opposed to the modern Choson period running from 1392 to 1910 C.E.

4 For that reason, *Dan Gun* is the name of the International Tae Kwon-Do Federation's (ITF) second pattern.

5 For this patriotic deed, *Moon Moo* is the name of the ITF's 21st pattern.

6 The 9th WTF form bears this name.

7 In his honor, the ITF's 23rd pattern is called *Sejong*.

8 Choi Hyong Un became known as *So San*, and his name is remembered in the ITF's 22nd pattern.

9 Admiral Yi was called *Choong Moo*, after whom the ITF's 9th pattern was named.

10 For very diverse descriptions of the *hwarang*, refer to Pieter (1994), and also Lee Joo Bang (2000).

11 Both *Yuk Ro* and *Ship Dan Kum* are names currently designating Soo Bahk Do forms recreated by Hwang Kee; *Du Mun* is the name of the first of the six *Yuk Ro* forms.

12 According to Hayes (1999-2000), seventh star of the Big Dipper (Ursa Major) that points to the North Star in the Little Dipper (Ursa Minor).

13 One of the advanced forms taught at the Korea Taekkyon Association is an empty handed sequence called *Yon Dan Sip Pal Soo*, which provokes more questions on the true origin of number 18 in Korean martial arts. Furthermore, Anne Loo (1984: 25) was introduced during her youth to "a Korean version of Shaolin gongfu called Sip Pal Ki Sorim Kwan in Korean." In China, Shaolin monks are said to have adopted 18 weapons from Tang Dynasty (618-907) officials before expanding their repertoire, and by the Song Dynasty (960-1279) referring to the "18 military weapons" had become common usage, these weapons subject to different listings according to the

different times and accounts. So the Shaolin connection remains a possible ancestor to some modern Korean Sip Pal Ki lineages, and would prove an alternative to the Sip Pal Ki of the *Muye Shinbo* military manuak

In connection with Taekkyon's barehanded Sip Pal form, it is hard to imagine a relation with a set of 18 weapons, either Korean or Chinese. In Chinese martial arts there exists the "18 hands of the enlightened" (ch. *Shi Ba Luo Han Shou*) taught by some as a martial art in itself (DeMarco, 2003), and by others as a set of exercises believed to preserve the roots of Bodhidharma/Damo's original teachings at the Shaolin Temple (López, 2002). Taekkyon seems to be closer to the shamanistic folk practices of inner Korea than to any Buddhist tradition, which would suggest that chances for it being related to Shaolin are slim. Still, a study of their similarities and differences and their historical relation, if any, awaits further research.

Glossary
Chinese Characters Listed by Korean Pronunciation

- Bon kuk kom: Indigenous sword of the country (Koreans referring to Silla's sword).
- Bong: Staff (j. *bo*).
- Chang: Spear.
- Choson: "Morning placid"; name for Korea during the Yi period (1392-1907). According to Samguk Yusa records of Korean legendary times, that was the original name Dan Gun adopted for his country in the 24th century B.C.E.
- Chuk Kye Kwang: Korean name for the Chinese author of the *Ki Hyo Shin Su*.
- Do: Blade, saber (j. *to*; ch. *dao*).
- Hankuk: The "Han" country/people. Korea. Reportedly meaning "bright/optimistic country/people".
- Hwarang: "Blossom/flower youth/boy." Organized group of young men in Silla during the 7th century. According to some accounts, it was a selected group of noble teenagers that received instruction in martial and fine arts and Buddhism to serve as officers in the country's army, resulting in heroic and ferocious deeds in battle. Traditionally, Korean martial art proponents have compared Korean Hwarang to Japanese samurai. For a revisionist perspective on the nature of the Hwarang, refer to Pieter (1994).
- Hyung: Form (ch. *xing*; j. *kata*).
- Jang kwon: Long fist/boxing (ch., *changquan*). Northern Chinese martial system that is believed to be the basis of the original Shaolin technique.
- Jeongjo: Korean king who ordered the preparation of the *Muye Dobo Tongji*.

- KOKURYO: Name of the largest realm (lasted from 37 B.C.E.-668 C.E.) of the Korean "Three Kingdoms Age."
- KOM SUL: Sword art/technique (j., *kenjutsu*). Although from the ideographic analysis "kom" refers to a double-edged blade, it became a generic term used for single-edged sabers as those used in medieval Japan.
- KON: Club (ch. *gun*; j. *kon*).
- KONG SU: "Empty hand" (ch. *kong shou*; j. *karate*), alternative characters to the original writing for "karate" adopted by Hanashiro Chomo and Funakoshi Gichin when such Okinawan art was introduced to the Japanese ethnocentric society of early 20th century.
- KORYO: Korean historical period from 927 to 1394.
- KUNG: Bow (j. *kyu*).
- KWON BOP: "Fist/boxing methods" (ch. *quanfa*; j, *kenpo*), the Korean version of the most widely used name for Chinese-derived weaponless martial arts in eastern Asia.
- MO WON UI: Korean name for the Chinese author of the *Mubiji*.
- MUBIJI: *Book of Military Preparation* (ch. *Wubeizhi*; j. *Bubiji*), Chinese 17th century manual written by Mao Yuanyi; also name of a southern Chinese White Crane boxing manual of unknown author, fundamental to Okinawan karate.
- MU DO JUNG SHIN: Righteous Spirit of the Martial Way.
- MU DOK KWAN (Moo Duk Kwan): "House of the Martial Virtue" (ch., *wu de quan*; j. *bu toku kan*). The name of Hwang Kee's dojang. For a serious treatment on the morality historically associated with Asian fist arts refer to Yang (1996).
- MUYE DOBO TONGJI: An illustrated martial arts manual written circa 1790 in Korea by Yi Dok Mu with collaboration of Park Je and Park Dong Su by order of King Jung Jo.
- PAEKCHE: Name of one of the "Three Kingdoms," which lasted from 18 B.C.E. to 660 C.E.
- PAL KAE: "Eight hexagrams" (ch., *bagua*). According to Daoism, the eight primary manifestations of the creative interaction of *um* and *yang* (ch., *yin* and *yang*) represented by hexagrams.
- PYON: Whip.
- SHIP PAL KI: "Eighteen Techniques." Name by which the *Muye Shinbo* Korean manual was popularly known. It currently identifies certain folk-derived Korean martial arts out of the mainstream styles.
- SILLA: Name of the smallest of the "Three Kingdoms" from 57 B.C.E. to 935 C.E.
- SORIM SA: "Little Forest Temple" (ch. *Shaolin Ssu*; j. *Shorin Ji*). Name of the monastery in Henan Province, China, in which Indian Buddhist missionary

Bodhidarma is believed to have introduced *Dyana* (j. *Zen*; ch. *Chan*; k. *Son*) around 530 C.E. and in which reportedly his yogic teachings merged with previous Chinese fighting methods creating a legendary martial art. Okinawan karate styles have kept this name.

- SUBAK: "Hitting hand" (ch., *shoubu*). Name used for weaponless martial arts in the Chinese-based *Muye Dobo Tongji*; also thought to be the name of ancient Korean barehand martial art (the characters shown correspond to those used in the *Muye Dobo Tongji*).

- TAE KUK: "Great principle" (ch., *taiji*; j., *tai kyoku*). According to Daoism, the underlying principle of existence. Adopted as the name for a Chinese martial art system.

- TAE KWON DO: "Way of the fist and feet." Name proposed by General Choi Hong Hi in 1955 to replace the *tang su / kong su* names that were used for karate derivatives in Korea. Along with this change, he proposed a number of technical modifications that in the aggregate resulted in a new martial art system which are believed to reflect many features of the Korean people.

- TAEKKYON: "To push shoulder." Taekkyon (also called *gak hi*, k.) is considered by many to be the only original, Korean martial art (Ouyang, 1997); proponents of this theory argue that the name has no associated Chinese characters. The characters shown (and respective meaning) are provided by Henning (2000), according to whom this martial art is also Chinese-related, and suggests the modern Korean pronunciation "Taek" replacing "Tak" may be the result of a deliberate or casual vocal change that suited supporters of Taekkyon's Korean origin. According to Pieter (1994), Chinese characters for *gak hi* are available, meaning "foot-play." It should be noted that present-day Taekkyon does not have any technical resemblance to any known Chinese martial art.

- TANG SU: "Tang (dynasty) hand"; "Chinese hand" (ch. *Tang shou*; ok. *Toudi*; j. *karate*), along with kenpo, was one of the names by which Chinese boxing became known in Okinawa.

- WAE KOM: Name ("foreign sword") used in *Muye Dobo Tongji* for the Japanese sword.

- WOL DO: Moon blade.

- YI DOK MU: Name of (Korean) author of the *Muye Dobo Tongji*.

- YON BI RYU: "Flying swallow lineage" (j., *Em Pi Ryu*). Ship Pal Ki family tradition inherited and led by Yoo Soo Nam from Argentina.

Bibliography

Capenter, S. (1995). *Problems in the identity and philosophy of T'aegwondo and their historical causes*. Available: www.bstkd.com/caoeber.1.htm.

Cho, Sihak H. (2000). *Tae Kwon Do: Secrets of Korean karate*. Tokyo: Tuttle.

Choi, Hong Hi. (1991). *Taekwon-Do. The Korean art of self-defense*. USSR: International Taekwon-Do Federation.

Chun, R. (1983). *Tae Kwon Do: El arte marcial Coreano*. Spanish language edition. New York: Harper & Row.

Clark, R. (1992). *Martial arts for the university. A textbook for basic judo, ju-jitsu, karate, Tae Kwon Do, Modern Arnis, and vital points*. Dubuque, IA: Kendall/Hunt Publishing Co.

Cook, H. (2001). *Shotokan karate: A precise history*. Thousand Oaks, CA: Dragon Times.

Cook, H. (April 1998). Ch'i Chi Kuang and the Chi Hsiao Hsin Shu. *Traditional Karate*.

Cook, H. (Summer 1999). The Bubishi. *Dragon Times*, #14.

Cremona, M. (November 2001). Personal interview with close quarters combat instructor and personal conditioning instructor of the Albatros Argentine special forces corps.

Della Pia, J. (1994). Korea's *Muyei Dobo Tongji*. *Journal of Asian Martial Arts*, 3(2), 62-71.

Della Pia, J. (1995). Native Korean sword techniques described in the *Mu Yae Do Bo Tong Ji*. *Journal of Asian Martial Arts*, 4(2), 86-97.

DeMarco, M. (2003). Taiwan, teachers and training: An interview with Yang Jwingming, Part II, *Journal of Asian Martial Arts*, 12(3), 74-88.

Gilbert, G. (May 1984). The evolution of the small weapons of China and their adoption by karate. *Karate Illustrated*.

Hanho (Sang H. Kim) (1992). *Combat strategy – Junsado: The way of the warrior*. Hartford, CT: Turtle Press.

Hayes, C. (Winter 1999/2000). Letter published in *World Moo Duk Kwan Newsletter*.

Henning, S. (2000). Traditional Korean martial arts. *Journal of Asian Martial Arts*, 9(1), 8-15.

Hsu, A. (n.d.). Entrenamiento mental: El arma secreta del Puño Largo. *Cinturón Negro*, Year XII, 123. Madrid: Budo International Publishing.

Hwang, K. (1978). *Tang Soo Do (Soo Bahk Do)*. Edited by the U.S. Tang Soo Do Moo Duk Kwan Federation.

Hwang, K. (1992). *Tang Soo Do Moo Duk Kwan, Volume 2*. Edited by the U.S. Tang Soo Do Moo Duk Kwan Headquarters.

Hwang, K. (1995). *The history of Moo Duk Kwan, celebrating the 50th anniver-

sary. Edited by Hwang Kee.

Hwang, Hyun Chul (December 1999). Personal interview with R. Longinotti. In, Sun Seo (1999). *Dae Han Ki Do Association* [On-line]. A general outline of martial arts and a brief history of Korean native martial arts. Available: http://www.kidohae.com/ history.htm.

Kang, Won Sik, and Lee, Kyong Myong, (n.d.). Modern history of Tae Kwon Do [On-line]. Available: http://www.martialartsresource.com/anonftp/ pub/the_dojang/digests /history.html.

Kim, Pyung Soo (1973). *Palgwe 1.2.3 of Tae Kwon Do hyung*. Los Angeles: Ohara Publications.

Kim, Sang H. (2000). *Mooye Dobo Tongji: The comprehensive illustrated manual of martial arts of ancient Korea*. Hartford, CT: Turtle Press.

Kim, Sang H. (June 2001). (Interview by Robert W. Young). Ancient wisdom: Korea's 211-year-old combat manual and its meaning for modern martial artists. *Black Belt*.

Kim, Sang H. (Sept. 2001). Korea's traditional weapons. *Tae Kwon Do Times*.

Kim, Un Yong (with Uhm Woon-kyu, Hong Chong-soo, Lee, Chong-woo, Han Seung-jo, Kim Young-hwan, Kim Soon-bae, Park Hae-man, et al.), (2000). *Kukkiwon Tae Kwon Do textbook*. Seoul: O Sung Publishing.

Kimm, He Young (1985). *Kuk Sool: Korean martial arts*. Louisiana: Andrew Jackson College Press.

Kimm, He Young (1985). *Han Mu Do: Korean intellectual martial arts*. Louisiana: Andrew Jackson College Press.

Kimm, He Young. (May 1999). Korea's oldest hand form: Kwon Bub Bo. *Tae Kwon Do Times*.

Kimm, He Young. (November 1997). Bon Kook Kum: Korean native sword form. *Tae Kwon Do Times*.

Lee, Joo Bang (July 2002). *World Hwa Rang Do Association* [On-line]. History and background of the art. Available: http://www.hwarangdo.com.

Lee, Ki Baik (1988). *Nueva historia de Corea*. (Spanish edition translated from *A New History of Korea*, 1st English edition, Ilchokak Publishers, Seoul, 1984) Buenos Aires: EUDEBA.

Lee, Kyong Myong (2001). *Taekwondo: Philosophy and culture*. Seoul: Hollym.

Lee, Yong Bok. (2001). *Taekkyon, videos I and II*. Hartford, CT: Turtle Press.

Loo, A. (Fall 1984). The need for Taekwon-do. *Traditional Taekwon-do*. pp. 25-26.

López, G. Garcia. (2002). Las manos de los dieciocho Luohan y las artes marciales. *Luohan Qigong* [On-line]. (The hands of the eighteen Luohan and the martial arts). Available: http://www.luohan.com/html_castellano /artemarcial_luohan.html.

McCarthy, P. (Trans.) (1996). *The bible of karate: Bubishi*. Tokyo: Tuttle.

Ouyang, Yung. (1997). The elevation of Taekkyon from folk game to martial art. *Journal of Asian Martial Arts*, 6(4), 76-89.

Park, Hae Man (November 2000). Personal interview.

Park, Joon Hyun (April 1980). Interview on Sipalki. *Yudo Karate Magazine* N° 75, pp. 32-33.

Pieter, W. (1994). Notes on the historical development of Korean martial sports. An addendum to Young's history and development of Tae Kyon. *Journal of Asian Martial Arts*, 3(1), 82-89.

Ratti, O. and Westbrook, A. (1994). *Los secretos del Samurai: Una investigación sobre las artes marciales del Japón feudal* (Spanish Edition translated from *Secrets of the samurai: A survey of the martial arts of feudal Japan*, Charles E. Tuttle, 1973) Madrid: Alianza Editorial.

Shim, Sang Kyu. (December 1997). Understanding the spirit of Tae Kwon Do through the history of Korea (Part I). *Tae Kwon Do Times*.

Shim, Sang Kyu. (January 1998). Understanding the spirit of Tae Kwon Do through the history of Korea (Part II, III, and IV). *Tae Kwon Do Times*.

Swift, J. (July 2002). *Fighting Arts.com* [On-line]. Roots of Shotokan: Funakoshi's original 15 kata, Parts I, II and III. Available: http://www.fightingarts.com.

World Jidokwan Federation. World Jidokwan Federation [On-line]. Jidokwan History. Available: http://www.worldjidokwan.co/history/th_history_of_jidokwan.html.

Yang, J. (1996). *The essence of Shaolin White Crane: Martial art power and qigong*. Jamaica Plain: YMAA.

Yoo, Soo Nam (n.d.). *Sipalki-do, el arte marcial de Corea*. Buenos Aires: Sempai Editora (M. Hladilo), Colección Yudo Karate.

Young, R. (1993). The history and development of Tae Kyon. *Journal of Asian Martial Arts*, 2(2), 44-67.

chapter 3

Korea's *Muye Dobo Tongji*
A Sample of Martial Arts Training in the Yi Dynasty

by John Della Pia, M.A.

Inside title page: "By Imperial Order — Muye Dobo Tongji."
Illustrations from the Muye Dobo Tongji courtesy of J. Della Pia.

In 1790, ChongJo (1776-1800), the twenty-second King of Korea's Yi Dynasty, ordered the compilation of a manual of martial arts for the royal army. The result was the *Muye Dobo Tongji*, or the *Illustrated Manual of Martial Arts*. Primarily a compilation of older works on the same subject, this document gives us a picture of the state of martial arts knowledge in Korea well before the turmoil of the nineteenth and twentieth centuries obscured much of Korea's culture and history. Many claims have been made as to the contents of the *Muye Dobo Tongji*. This chapter will give some background on the author and his sources and then an overview of the book and some translations from the empty-hands chapter of volume four.

Yi Dok Mu (1741-1794), author of the *Muye Dobo Tongji*, was a government official well known as a scholar, poet, calligrapher, and martial artist. He had travelled to Beijing and was especially noted for his knowledge of rare Chinese classics, a knowledge he demonstrates in his book. At the time

44

Lee compiled the *Muye Dobo Tongji*, he was part of a large group of scholars King ChongJo had gathered at the palace in his newly established research library. They were tasked to produce works on a wide variety of practical subjects. New castings of metal type were prepared especially for their works using examples from the finest Korean and Chinese calligraphers.

It was the standard for Korean scholars of Lee's time to follow the Chinese example in writing as set down centuries before. The text of his work is in classical literary Chinese and does not use the native Korean alphabet. The author was expected to use numerous examples from classical texts and then add his own comments, which Lee did. This gave to the work an authority that would have been totally lacking had Lee tried to present a document based solely on his own writing. In his introduction Lee listed over one hundred classic Chinese, Korean, and even Japanese works. A partial listing of titles may give some idea as to how much research went into this book. (Note that some of these are many volumes long themselves.)

- *Complete History of the Tang*
- *Complete History of the Northern Song*
- *Complete History of the Song*
- *The Three Kingdoms*
- *The Books of the Early Han*
- *The Books of the Later Han*
- *Songs of the Dragons Flying to Heaven*
- *The Writings of Confucius and Mencius*
- *Internal Style Boxing*
- *Shaolin Style Roots and Methods*
- *New Text of Practical Tactics*

In addition to those I have listed, Lee cited many more texts on history, poetry, martial arts, weapons, horsemanship, and warfare. Lee also made a point in his introduction of giving credit to Qi Jiguang and Mao Yuanyi, Chinese authors quoted extensively in each volume. Qi Jiguang's *New Text of Practical Tactics* was used for training the Korean armies before the *Muye Dobo Tongji* was introduced.

The *Muye Dobo Tongji* consists of four volumes and an introductory section. The first volume has chapters on the long spear; flag spear; trident spear; use of the spear from horseback; and the "wolf brush," a vicious looking, long bamboo spear with eleven side-blades all pointing forward. Each of these weapons is illustrated and a prearranged form (Kr., *hyung*; Jap. *kata*) is included for each one.

Volume two is on the sword and contains chapters explaining the two-handed sword; the pointed sword, showing illustrations of several Chinese and Korean swords; and the Japanese sword. There are prearranged forms for each weapon including a two-person sparring set included at the end of the volume.

Volume three is divided into chapters on drawing the sword, the basic use of the sword, the use of two swords, the "moon sword" (a wide-blade halberd), narrow-blade halberd, sword and shield. Illustrations are included for each along with forms and techniques for using the weapons from horseback.

Volume four contains chapters on empty-handed fighting; the staff (or bo); the battle flail, which is a staff connected by a length of chain or rope to a shorter stick; the use of this weapon from horseback; "ball striking" (polo); trick riding; and the clothing and armor worn by both mounted and foot soldiers. There are descriptions of two-person fighting sets in the chapter on empty-hand fighting, and the staff, and a description of the battle flail used against the staff.

Left: The use of twin swords from horseback.
Right: Polo player utilizing battlefield skills.

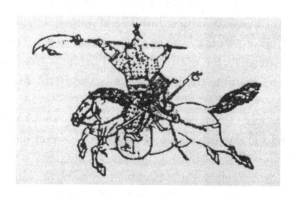

Wielding the moon sword from horseback.

Martial postures illustrated in chapter one, volume four
of the *Muye Dobo Tongji*. The Chinese characters read
"*quanfa pu*," meaning "examples of boxing methods."

Chapter one of volume four, which deals with empty-hand fighting, starts off with a general introduction:

> Qi Jiguang stated that kwon bop "fist methods" do not resemble skills used in great battles (as between armies). However, diligent activity of the hands and feet is the door to making the body graceful.

The term "*kwon bop*" is the title of the first chapter of volume four and is found on every page of that chapter. "Fist methods" is one possible translation; "boxing" yet another. Most American readers will be more familiar with "kempo," the Japanese pronunciation of these same two Chinese characters, or with the Chinese "*quanfa.*"

Lee compares mastering the basics in martial arts to learning to use a writing brush or to riding a horse:

> Mao Yuanyi stated "know the dots and strokes and after that one can learn the eight methods [of brush writing]." In [the book] *Calligraphy Circles*, it is stated that Wang Gil So first learned to master the "eternal" character's eight strokes and then had the ability to write in eight methods.

(The character for "eternal" when done in the old classic style used eight strokes considered basic to writing with a brush.)

> One must first know how to saddle a horse before one can learn to ride swiftly. It is the same when speaking of using the fist.

Next Lee comments on the use of stances in martial arts:

[The book] *Military Volume* states that the person who has power because of "fist methods" knows stances and knows how to use change, [such as] turning sideways, standing upright, running and dropping low [on one's belly], It is like having a wall around one's house and using it to both defend and to attack. Therefore, when speaking of kwon bop, the person who knows the stances uses no fixed stance, but changes to whatever stance is suitable. He has no stance but does not lose his stance. The poem "Small Refinement" says without knowledge of kwon bop one will have difficulty being courageous. The study of kwon bop will develop strength.

Martial postures illustrated in chapter one, volume four of the *Muye Dobo Tongji*.

Lee continues to quote from various Chinese classics, mentions stories of great feats of legendary martial artists, and goes into a short history of martial arts development in China. The following are some of the more interesting highlights:

From the [time of] the Tang and Song [Dynasties], there are two types of techniques. One is the external family and one is the internal family. The external family comes from Shaolin.

Lee adds a footnote here:

The Shaolin Temple existed in Deng Feng County, Shaoshi Mountain. The *Daily Records* [of that county] state that at the beginning of the Tang [Dynasty] thirteen temple monks suppressed Wang Shizhong, bringing victory [to the Tang Dynasty] thus came about the Shaolin soldiers. A Shaolin monk was given command and ordered to defend against Japanese pirates at the Song River [where] many were killed. Therefore [Shaolin] thrived.

Next he quotes from a document on internal family methods:

Internal family is correctly attributed to Zhang Songxi. Songxi taught thirteen students methods from the Song [Dynasty] Wudang Mountain Daoist Zhang Sanfeng.

Lee claims (or quotes authorities who claim) that the Shaolin techniques cause too much exertion and movement on the part of the practitioner, giving an advantage to the enemy, while (again quoting from an internal-style family document):

Songxi's technique was to defend and not go out to the enemy until there was an opening. [But] once used [the technique] was effective. Therefore, the internal-style family technique is better. The striking person [*pak in*] needs [to know] the points that exist. Dizzying points, dumb points, death points, mutual points and both light and heavy strikes to cause death, dizziness and dumbness without the slightest mistake.

There are two terms here that are interesting. Lee uses (or quotes) the term "*pak in*" for striking person. Earlier in the text, he also uses the *pak* character in the term "*soo pak*," or striking hand, as a term for empty-handed martial arts. The second term of interest is "points." Lee uses the same term as is used in acupuncture for body points. (Acupuncture was firmly established in Korea centuries before Lee's time.)

Most of the kwon bop chapter in volume four is taken up by illustrations and text describing the two-person fighting set or form. Understanding even a modern day written explanation of the actual movements in a no prearranged form is difficult. Deciphering Lee's sparse, classical sentences is much more difficult. To give the interested reader some idea of what this form was like I have included a translation of the starting movements to the two-person set, which starts on page six:

> Both men chamber their hands at the waist and stand in a horse-stance.
> The right hand strikes open [towards] the left shoulder.
> Turn into a "phoenix elbow" stance.
> The left hand strikes open [towards] the right shoulder.
> Without weight on the leg, take an "empty fodder" stance.
> The right foot kicks to the left hand.
> The left foot kicks to the right hand.
> Go immediately into a "phoenix elbow" stance.
> Pivot to the left and kick the left hand with the right foot.

1) wolf brush, 2) twin swords, 3) flag spear, 4) flail against a staff.
Martial postures illustrated in chapter one, volume four of the *Muye Dobo Tongji*.

One modern-day martial artist who has spent years studying this section of the *Muye Dobo Tongji* is Tangsudo 's founder, Hwang Kee. He states in the introduction to his book *Tang Soo Do Moo Duk Kwan, Vol. III*:

> In 1957, I was delighted to discover, for the first time, the [Mu] Yei Dobo
> Tongji at the Seoul National University Library. It was a truly remarkable
> moment for me since my entire life, since childhood, has been dedicated
> to the martial arts.

Man armed with a moon-sword.

Hwang Kee, in a September, 1993, interview with the *Cho Son II Bo* newspaper in Seoul, states that, based on this discovery, he changed the name of the Korean branch of his association to Soo Bahk (Pak) Do in June, 1960, and spent the next thirty years interpreting the empty-hands section of the *Muye Dobo Tongji* into forms. Today he has completed a series of forms based on this research.

In view of the claims by each of the various Korean martial arts to be the one true "Korean" art, I would like to try to place the *Muye Dobo Tongji* in some perspective. While this priceless historical document gives us a chance to examine the state of martial arts in Korea over two hundred years ago, it does not attempt to show a unique Korean art. It was intended to provide information on martial arts for the benefit and training of the army, and to that end, Lee Du'k Mu used all possible sources, most of which were Chinese. While the term "Mu Ye" translated directly to "martial art," most of the book explains skills that were to be used in actual warfare, subjects that today would be classified as military science.

It is a rare book on Korean martial arts published today that does not at least mention the *Muye Dobo Tongji*. Some go so far as to insert the word "Korean" into the title when translating it into English. Lee Du'k Mu, writing over one hundred years before the tragic years of the Japanese occupation, felt no such compulsion. In a book of nearly three hundred pages, only sixteen deal with empty-hand fighting and most of the quoted sources in this section are Chinese. With the exception of Hwang Kee's modern interpretations noted above, none of the martial arts taught as "Korean" today can show a direct connection to this book. This in no way should diminish its value and interest to martial arts practitioners and scholars studying now. The book does show clearly that Korean martial artists of the 1700's used prearranged forms and two-person fighting sets and studied weak points of the body, possibly based on acupuncture points. They were familiar with a large variety of weapons and practiced forms with them. All of this indicates serious, advanced martial arts training. The book warrants further study and translations of some of the other chapters because the rewards would shed great light on the development of martial arts in Korea.

Bibliography

Hwang, K. (1970). *Subak do dae gam*. Seoul, Korea: Han Uri.

Hwang, K. (1992). *Tang soo do (soo bahk do) moo duk kwan*. Springfield, NJ: Private printing.

Lee, K. B. (1976). *A new history of Korea*. Cambridge, MA: Harvard University Press.

Lee, S. G. (1978). *Tae han guk sa*. Seoul, Korea: Sin Tae Yang Sa.

Lee, B. T. (1959). *Myong shi chon s'o*. Seoul, Korea: Mun Ho'n P'yon Chan Hui.

Mathews, R. H. (1963). *Mathew's Chinese-English dictionary*. Cambridge, MA: Harvard University Press.

Note

When transliterating Korean words into English the two most common systems are McCune-Reischauer and "Seoul Standard," which up until recently was promoted by the Republic of Korea Ministry of Education. McCune-Reischauer is more readily pronounceable by native English speakers and I much prefer it. When using our alphabet to write Korean words, names in particular, it is easy for a reader to be misled. That there are two transliteration systems is partially to blame for this, but there are other reasons as well. Yi Dok Mu, for example, is called Lee Dok Mu in some English language references and Yi Duk Mu in others. I have tried to use the most common versions of the spelling for the names and terms regardless of the transliteration systems. Including the Chinese characters removes much of the guesswork, so I have included a list of terms and names which appear in this chapter. These are as found in the *Muye Dobo Tongji* and may not match exactly with other historical documents. Wherever a source or name was clearly Chinese, I transliterated it in its Chinese rather than Korean form. Thus, "Zhang Songxi" is used rather than "Chang Song Kye," which is the Korean pronunciation of the same Chinese characters. Where I had some question as to the nationality, I left the transliteration in the Korean version.

Terminology

English	Korean	Mandarin	Chinese
Illustrated Manual of Martial Arts	*Muye Dobo Tongji*	Wu³ Yi² Tu⁴ Pu³ Tong¹ Zhi⁴	武藝圖譜 通志
form	hyung	xing⁴	形
moon sword	—	yue² dao¹	月刀
(person's name)	Lee Du'k Mu	Li³ De⁴-mao²	李德懋
(person's name)	—	Qi¹ Ji²-guang¹	戚繼光
(person's name)	—	Mao⁴ Yuan⁴-yi⁴	茅元儀
boxing method	kwon bop	quan⁴ fa³	拳法
(person's name)	—	Zhang¹San¹-feng1	張三丰
(person's name)	Chang Song Kye	Zhang¹ Song¹-xi¹	張松溪
"striking person"	pak in	bo³ ren⁴	搏人
"striking hand"	soo pak/pahk	shou³ bo³	手搏
points	—	xue⁴	穴
death points	—	si³ xue⁴	死穴

53

chapter 4

Native Korean Sword Techniques Described in the *Muye Dobo Tongji*

by John Della Pia, M.A.

An opponent's view of
"Coiling and Thrusting."
*Photos and illustrations
courtesy of J. Della Pia.*

The sword has a long history in Korea, some Korean martial artists claiming sword techniques unique to the peninsula were developed even before the start of the Three Kingdoms period (traditional dates 57 B.C.E.-935 C.E.). Korea's oldest surviving martial arts text, the *Muye Dobo Tongji* (1790), makes an intriguing case for this position, presenting a subsection on the "Native Sword" and including a prearranged form with postures stated to have originated at least partially in Korea. The purpose of this chapter is to explore this claim while giving the modern martial artist a glimpse of past weapons training native to Korea.

Before presenting a translation of the "Native Sword" section of the *Muye Dobo Tongji*, some background notes are in order to help clarify the text. First, the compilers used three Chinese characters to identify different sections of the text: "original," "additional," and "documentation." Each of these appears before the text as a white character outlined with a black border. "Original" precedes text from an older primary source, usually earlier training manuals. "Additional" precedes material unique to the *Muye Dobo Tongji*, and "documentation" signifies supporting material added to improve understanding. I have prefaced each translated section with these same terms, making it possible to see what material came from Chinese sources and what material is unique to the *Muye Dobo Tongji*.

Second, the "Mao" and "Qi" regularly quoted and referred to in the text are Mao Yuanyi and Qi Jiguang, famous Ming Dynasty (1368-1644) Chinese generals who wrote texts on warfare and the martial arts. These texts were well known and widely used in Korea. Finally, the names of the postures shown for the form are clearly Chinese. However, in the general overview of the book the compilers state that, even though the postures did not match Mao Yuanyi's original work, they used his terminology. This was done because "Mao's work had set the standard for all future works."

NATIVE SWORD
A Translation of the Foreword

Additional

Commonly called "new sword," this is a waist sword as is the pointed sword. It is said in the *Yo Ji Su'ng-nam* that Hwang Chang Rang was a man of Shilla. According to folklore, he went to Paekche at the age of seven, and so many people came to watch him dance in the marketplace it seemed as if a wall had formed. The King of Paekche heard of this and commanded that he perform for the court. Chang Rang took this opportunity to stab the king. The people then killed him. Shilla grieved and made a dance-mask in the likeness of his face to use in the sword dance. This was passed down to today.

Documentation

Hwang Cheng ("Yellow-actor") was also known as Hwang Chang ("Yellow-prosperity"). He is of the Hwarang of Shilla. (The people of Shilla found no obstacle too great in finding a person with proper requirements for services required. They took the most beautiful boys and dressed them with ornaments. These were called Hwarang. People gathered like clouds and the honest could be seen and selected from the deceitful.) Sul Rang and Yong Rang (legend says Sul Rang, Nam Rang, and Yong Rang played at the Chonso'k Pavillion in Tongcho'n, Ansang) were of this lineage. Hwang Chang Rang was also one of these. There were thousands of Hwarang who polished and sharpened their loyalty and fidelity. Shilla sent their dancing sword-boys to neighboring countries where they were not watched too closely. Thus it is from Hwang Chang Rang the native sword is said to have originated.

Mao Yuanyi may have obtained some sword text from Korea. When compared to the western frontier area, Korea had a native sword text with original ideas. In Japanese historical texts, it is stated that Korea added original material to the text from China. Some of the material is original, some handed down. From now back to Mao's time is one hundred plus years. Those who directly received the resulting text were not few in number. We can not know if native people freely transmitted, received or knew of Mao's *Mubishi*. Some day this may be known but for the above reasons and with apologies to Mao, the following is presented as "Native Sword Text."

A form of Sword Dance exists even today in Korea but in a clearly watered-down version. As late as 1900, however, there was evidence of powerful techniques still preserved in the dance. William Franklin Sands, an American advisor to the Korean Emperor up until the beginning of the Japanese takeover, describes a sword dance performed as part of a village wedding celebration:

> Inside the house of Kisang, dancing girls went through their classic Flower Dance, a sword dance representing some very old legend, obscured by the mists of time, of the attempted assassination of some great man. An enemy, not daring to attack him openly, gives a banquet and bribes a famous sword dancer to show his skill with a real sword, meaning of course to bring about an accident. A retainer of the guest, suspecting treachery but not daring to accuse so great a person as the host, takes up a sword and joins in the dance, interposing himself always with the greatest skill and grace between his master and the assassin. Both the guest and the host become aware of what is happening, but, Korean-like, are lost in admiration of the skill of the duelists who wage a deadly battle under the guise of play. Neither must permit the real object of the contest to appear, for, the principals, being great gentlemen, there mustn't be even the slightest infraction of court etiquette, even in a murder. Of course the murderer sinks exhausted and the guest is saved. Korean tales always turn out the right way, for virtue is always rewarded.

Next I would like to examine the "Native Sword" section itself. This consists of a form divided into thirty-four postures or stances. In the original book, each page containing illustrations was divided halfway down into an upper and lower section. The upper section contained text and the lower section contained two figures illustrating the postures described in the text above.

In addition, the book was opened and read from right to left and this is also the way the illustrations were arranged, the figure on the right being first. As there are only twenty-four figures illustrated, not all of the postures described are shown. It would be impossible to follow this form using only these drawings.

Fortunately there are three more pages provided which make it possible to decipher this puzzle. The first is a map of where and in which direction each posture is being performed. The name of each posture is written inside a black border. The characters are read in the direction the practitioner would face if actually performing the form. The second and third pages are composite drawings of all thirty-four postures showing the posture, direction of movement and any turns or pivots being performed. In the general overview, the compilers state that all such maps and composite drawings are done to scale. Also, when the text states "using the right foot" or "using the left foot," this seems to indicate in the corresponding drawing which foot is weight bearing, not which foot is forward.

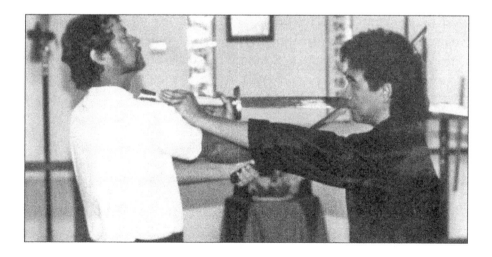

Photo shows that
"Right Needle Attack"
is actually a
butt-stroke to the face
using the sword hilt (Fig. 21).

NATIVE SWORD TEXT

Original

- Fig. 1: First assume the "Hold the Sword, Face the Thief." Both hands grasp the hilt. Stand erect with the sword at the left shoulder.
- Fig. 2: Turn to the right. The right foot turns, brushing past on the inside.
- Fig. 3: Next do "Advance Forward to Attack the Thief." Using the right hand and right leg, strike forward.
- Fig. 4: Assume a "Golden Rooster Stands on One Leg." Lift the sword and the left leg. Turn to the left and face to the rear.
- Fig. 5: Turning to the left, do a "Rear Single Strike." Using the right hand and right leg, strike once.
- Fig. 6: Assume a "Golden Rooster Stands on One Leg." Turn to the left, raise the sword and left leg, turn and look forward.
- Turning to the left assume "Advance Forward to Attack the Thief."
- Immediately coil left and right. Using the left hand and left leg, thrust once.
- Fig. 7: Next assume "Wild Tiger Hides in the Forest." Turn twice to the right.
- Fig. 8: Turn to the left into "Wild Goose Character." Facing the right side, coil left and right. Using the right hand and left foot, thrust once.
- Fig. 9: Assume "Zhi-fu Sends the Scroll." Turning (from the right) and using the right hand and left leg, thrust once to the left side.
- Fig. 10: Turning to the left, face forward and assume "Part the Grass, Search for the Snake." Using the right hand and right foot, hit once. With one foot, advance, taking a jumping step.
- Fig. 11: Assume "Press the Leopard's Forehead." Coil left and right. Using the right hand and right foot, thrust forward once.

- Fig. 12: From there turn to the right. Turn to the rear and assume an "Early Sky." With both hands hold the sword at forehead level. Turning right, turn and advance facing to the rear.
- Fig. 13: Do an "Insert Animal Head."
- Fig. 14: From there assume a "Face Right, Block the Thief." Lift the left leg and brush by to the outside.
- Do "Rear Single Attack." Using the right hand from the right leg, strike once.
- Fig. 15: Turn to the right and face forward. Assume "Spread the Flag." Lift the right leg and brush by the inside.
- From there do "Advance Forward, Kill the Thief." Using the right hand and right leg, strike once.
- Next do "Golden Rooster Stands on One Leg." Raise the blade high, raise the left leg, turn and look to the rear.
- Fig. 16: Next turn to the left and do "Left Waist Attack." Lift the leg, and with the sword on the left side, wash the left side of the neck.
- Fig. 17: Immediately turn to the right and perform "Right Waist Attack." Lift the right leg, and with the sword on the right side, wash the right side of the neck.
- Fig. 18: Immediately turn to the right and do "Rear Single Thrust." Using the right hand and left foot, thrust once.
- Fig. 19: Turn to the left, face forward and do "Long Dragon Spouts Water." Strike once using the right hand and right foot.
- Fig. 20: Next do "White Ape Departs the Cave." Raise the right hand and right foot.

- Fig. 21: Do "Right Needle Attack." Twist the right hand, step with the right leg, and thrust hard to the right.
- Fig. 22: Turning to the right, assume "Bravely Skip, Single Thrust." With the right hand and left leg, thrust once.
- Turn to the left and face the rear. Do "Rear Single Strike." Strike once using the right hand and right leg.
- From there move into "Rear Single Thrust." Coil left and right. Using the right hand and left leg, thrust once.
- Fig. 23: Next turn to the right and face forward. Do "Face Right and Block the Thief." Raise the left foot and brush to the outside.
- Immediately assume "Face Front and Kill the Thief." Using the right hand and right leg, strike twice to the front.
- Fig. 24: Next do "Rhinoceros and Ox Face-Off in Battle." Using the right hand and left leg, thrust once and finish.

The final two pages of the "Native Sword" section (Figs. 25 and 26) present the entire form drawn to scale, showing the direction of movement, number of turns, and individual postures. This method of presentation is followed throughout the book.

We can draw some conclusions about Korean sword techniques based on the comments made in the *Muye Dobo Tongji*. We learn that a unique Korean style of sword and swordmanship have been used on the peninsula for at least the past two thousand years. The swords were still being used as late as 1790 as part of the regular equipment issued to Korean troops.

Native techniques were influenced by Chinese masters and texts, especially the works of Qi Jiguang and Mao Yuanyi, but there is a strong case to be made for native origin of Korean techniques as well. The form shown above was used for serious training by men who expected to be called upon to use the sword to defend coastal towns and villages against the incessant Japanese pirate raids of that period. Training under those conditions took on a literal life or death meaning for the trainee. The postures and movements shown and described were combat-tested and proven techniques, nothing flashy, nothing acrobatic, nothing made up for show. They provide clear evidence of sophisticated weapons training in Korea well before the Japanese occupation in 1910.

Today in the Republic of Korea, there is a great resurgence of interest in the arts and culture suppressed during the occupation. Many arts previously thought lost have reappeared, secretly recorded or passed on orally by a few practitioners. Native sword techniques may well be among them.

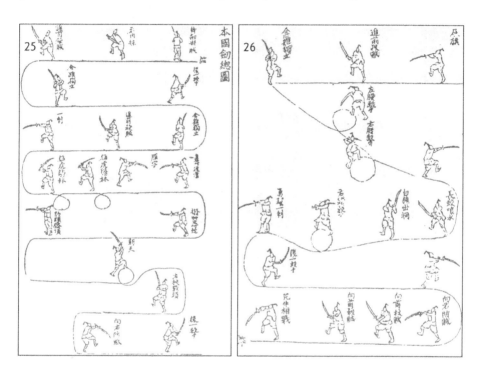

MODERN INTERPRETATION

Even modern martial art books can be hard to follow unless one is already familiar with the subject matter. For help in understanding the postures shown and described in this section of the *Muye Dobo Tongji*, I approached Grandmaster Johnny Kwong Ming Lee, lineage holder of the Northern Shaolin style of My Jhong Law Horn. From previous contact, I knew Master Lee to be very familiar with the writings of both Qi Jiguang and Mao Yuanyi. The postures shown in the *Muye Dobo Tongji* were familiar to him and it took him only a few minutes, sword in hand, to turn the old drawings into smooth, deadly movements.

The following is Master Lee's demonstration of some of the postures as illustrated and described in the original text.

Photo 1: shows "Brushing Past on the Right," which simulates drawing the sword and blocking an attack (Fig. 2).

Photo 2: shows "Golden Rooster Stands on One Leg," which first blocks the opponent's downward strike and then is followed up with a downward strike of one's own (Fig. 4).

Photo 3: shows "Rear Single Strike," which looks the
same today as it did two hundred years ago (Fig. 5).

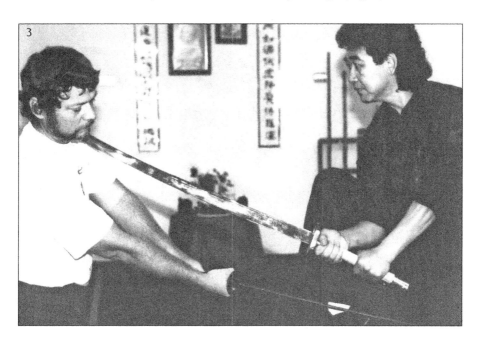

Photo 4: shows "Zui-fu Sends the Scroll," in which one's sword guides
the opponent's sword out and away before thrusting inward (see Fig. 9).

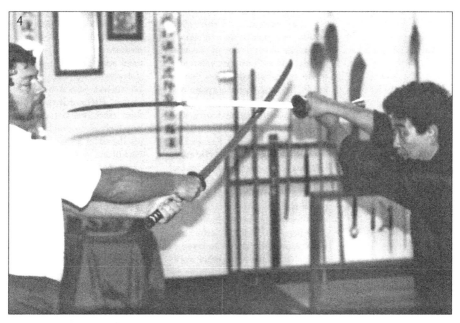

- Photo 5: shows "Right Needle Attack," is actually a butt-stroke to the face using the sword hilt (Fig. 21).
- Photo 6: shows an opponent's view of "Coiling and Thrusting."

Finally, on the question of the origin of the techniques, Master Lee suggests that the question is unanswerable.

These techniques have been known in China for over five hundred years and in Korea as well. Should you somehow survive facing an enemy who demonstrates techniques superior to yours, you take them for your own. If he has a better weapon, you copy it and improve on it or make something to counter it. Martial artists and warriors five hundred or one thousand years ago didn't care if the technique was native or not, only if it would help them win and live. How could we say where each movement originated?

Bibliography

Lee, K. B. (1976). *A new history of Korea*. Cambridge, MA: Harvard University Press.

Lee, S. G. (1978). *Tae han guk sa*. Seoul, Korea: Sin Tae Yang Sa.

Sands, W. F. (1987). *At the court of Korea*. London: Century Hutchinson Ltd.

chapter 5

Increased Lung Capacity
Through Qigong Breathing Techniques
of the Chung Moo Martial Art Style

by Patrick Massey, M.D., Ph.D., and Eugene Thorner, M.D.,
William L. Preston, M.D., & John S. Lee, M.D.

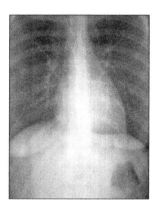

X-Ray of a twenty-two year old female.

Introduction

There are many reports of the healthful benefits of martial art training (Zhao, 1984; Maliszewski, 1992). Usually these reports consist of martial art experts, as well as students, attesting to the value of their training programs. These benefits can include improved physical fitness, resolution of specific body problems and a subjective feeling of mental improvement. However, objective evidence on the effectiveness of martial art training for improving the health of the average student is lacking.

Martial art training involves the performance of specific movements over a period of time until a certain proficiency is achieved. One important aspect of many advanced martial art training programs involves the development of some form of breathing control. Specific breathing forms (*qigong*) have been alleged to improve the circulation and strengthen both the immune system and the internal organs. Other qigong breathing forms stretch the muscles, clear the mind and reduce stress (Eisenberg, 1985; Wilhelm, 1985). Qigong means the practice of developing qi. Qi has been described as the energy of the body. It is associated with breathing as well as muscle and mental activity. It is more of a life energy than a measurable substance (Ming-Dao, 1990).

Qiqong breathing techniques are taught in the Chung Moo style of martial art. *Chung* (mind) *Moo* (body) martial art (also known as *UmYang* martial arts) has its foundation in Chinese martial arts. It was first introduced into the United States twenty years ago.

Our own positive experiences practicing qigong breathing (a cumulative experience of twenty-nine years in the Chung Moo style of martial art) led us to interview many other students who also practice qigong breathing forms. They stated that they felt "energized" after practicing qigong breathing and they were able to complete daily activities more easily. Many stated that they had fewer colds, more energy and greater endurance. Some of these students originally had been severe, activity-restricted asthmatics. After practicing qigong breathing, they became very active and also noticed a marked decrease in the use of their asthma medications (Massey and Thorner, 1992).

We wanted to determine if there was a measurable, physiologic parameter that could justify the apparent feeling of improved health in those practicing qigong breathing. Since the students were practicing a specific breathing form, the most obvious parameter to measure was the amount of air each student could exhale with a single breath. We postulated that, through qigong breathing techniques, there may be a significant increase in the lung capacity. We compared the functional lung capacity in those students who practiced qigong breathing with the lung capacities of an age- and height-matched control population (national average). Our data confirmed that students who practiced qigong breathing had a marked increase in their lung capacity.

Methods

One hundred students training in the Chung Moo style of martial art volunteered to participate in this study. Students were randomly selected and represent an age span of between twenty and seventy-one years of age. All had been practicing qigong breathing forms for at least four months.

The lung capacity of each student was measured using an Assess Peak Flow Spirometer. Students, after taking a deep breath, would expel as much air as possible, as fast as possible into the spirometer. The flow of air (liter/min.) was measured by the spirometer. Spirometry was performed four consecutive times per student. All students were evaluated before practicing qigong breathing forms. The numeric value for each student was determined as the average of the four attempts. The numeric value of each age group was an average of all of the students in that age group.

The numeric value of lung capacity was calculated by using the national standards for lung capacity and peak air flow volumes. Since lung capacity is directly related to both age and height, student's lung capacities were compared with national averages for both their age and height (Leiner, et al., 1963).

A Sample Qigong Breathing Technique
Photos courtesy of E. Thorner.

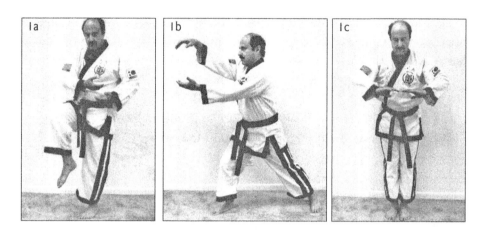

Figure 1a: Air is drawn into the lungs through the nose as the arms and leg move to one side in unison. **Figure 1b:** Intake of air is completed as the arms reach the level of the shoulders. The air is then pushed into the abdomen, ready for expulsion. **Figure 1c:** Air is released in a controlled manner as the arms move downward.

Figure 1d: The movement is completed with total release of the air, an extension of the arms toward the toes and a pulling in of the stomach. The entire sequence can then be repeated.

Results

Figure 1: Qigong breathing practiced by students in the Chung Moo style of martial art. One of many different qigong breathing forms is demonstrated. Air is taken in through the nose (Figs. 1-a and b), forced down into the abdominal area (Fig. 1-c) and finally expelled through the mouth while contracting the abdomen (Figs. 1-c and d). These and other similar breathing movements are practiced for twenty minutes per day, three to four times a week. Movements are done in a relaxed manner and are continuous. Qigong breathing movements are done an equal number of times on the right and left side.

FIGURE II
Increased Peak Flow Rate in Students Practicing
Qigong Breathing in the Chun Moo-Style of Martial Art

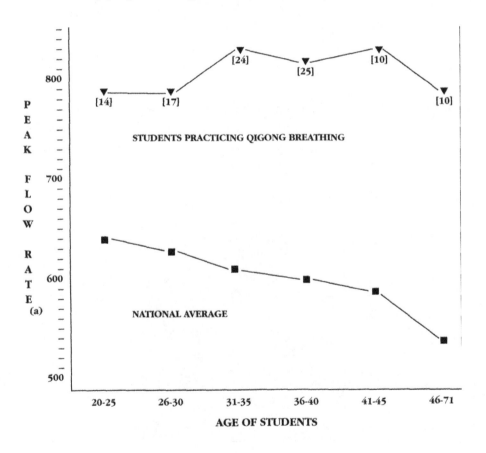

(a) Liters of air per minute

[ ] Number of students per age group

Increased peak flow rate in students practicing qigong breathing in the Chung Moo style of martial art. The peak flow for each age group represents the maximum speed at which air was expelled from the lungs after a single deep breath. Each value is the average of four measurements for each student in the specific age group. These values were compared to the national average for each age group. The national average peak air flow declines with increasing age. In comparison, there was no decline in the peak air flow for those students between the ages of twenty and seventy-one who practiced qigong breathing.

FIGURE III
Percent Increase in Lung Capacity of Students Practicing Qigong Breathing in the Chun Moo-Style of Martial Art

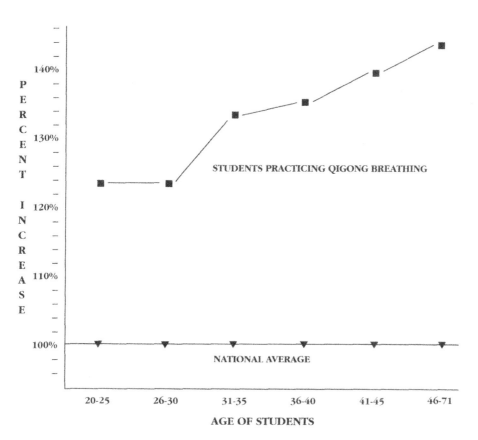

Percent increase in the lung capacity of students practicing qigong breathing in the Chung Moo martial art style. These data show that the greatest percent increase in lung capacity is in the older students (between thirty-six and seventy-one years of age) who practiced qigong breathing. For comparison purposes, the national average lung capacity for each age group was set at 100%. As a result, in the older students, the lung capacities were 30-45% greater than age and height-matched controls (national average). A smaller but significant increase over the national average (20-25%) was seen in the younger students.

Discussion

As the human body ages, certain functions diminish. There is a decrease in hearing, eyesight, muscle mass, bone density, memory and learning. Reaction time dramatically increases. There is also a decrease in lung capacity that is believed to be irreversible (Poppy, 1992). This loss of lung capacity may reflect structural changes of the chest shape resulting from increased curvature of the spine and a loss of postural height (most commonly the result of osteoporosis). There are also changes in the lung tissue itself. The lung tissue loses some of its elasticity. This is the result of years of scarring by multiple insults to the lung tissue, e.g, exposure to toxins in our environment: pollution and tobacco smoke. Scarring will also occur as the result of the immune response to infections (pneumonia) and allergens (asthma). As the amount of scarring increases, the lung tissue becomes less flexible (like a dry balloon). The measurable result of a stiff lung is a decreased lung volume. Although antioxidants and specific aerosolized enzymes do hold promise in some specific lung diseases, this is not applicable to the general population; there are no drugs that can stay the ravages of time (Hubbard, et al. 1989). In other words, the loss of lung function is not believed to be reversible to any great degree. It is simply an unfortunate result of the inevitable aging process.

The practice of martial arts emphasizes that loss of function may not be permanent and that through the proper training, the aging process can be slowed. There are many examples of older martial art students who can perform physical tasks as well as someone many years younger (Min Dao, 1990 and Maliszewski, 1992). We documented that the practice of qigong breathing techniques made many students subjectively more energetic, increased their stamina. However, we were interested in objectively documenting if this feeling of increased stamina was related to any physical changes in the students. The most obvious place to start was to measure lung capacity.

Qigong may have been originally introduced into Chinese martial arts by various Daoist groups. These breathing techniques were greatly enriched in the Tang Dynasty by the incorporation of breathing forms traditionally introduced to the Chinese by the Indian Buddhist monk Bodhidharma. Eventually, qigong movements found their way into many Chinese martial art forms (Ming-Dao, 1990). Qigong incorporates many different positions and movements and is most often associated with promotion of health through the development of internal strength (Chang, 1978). These breathing techniques are so intertwined with Chinese martial arts that now it is almost impossible to practice advanced martial art forms without being introduced to some form of qigong breathing.

We wanted to evaluate the effects of qigong breathing on the lung capacity. We needed a large group of participants who were all practicing the same set of breathing movements. In this way the individual results from each age group could be combined. We chose to evaluate students practicing the Chung Moo style of martial art. The Chung Moo style has deep roots in Chinese martial arts and specific qigong breathing forms are part of the training program. Chung means a "balanced mind" and Moo means a "strong body." Chung Moo, a name used generally throughout Asia, can also represent the aspects of *Yin* and *Yang* (Chinese) or *Um Yang* (Korean), signifying a balance between the mind and the body.

Practice of the qigong breathing movements involves a controlled intake of a large volume of air into the lungs. The air is then pushed into the abdominal area and then is followed by a controlled expelling of the air (Fig. I). Our data confirmed the hypothesis that there was a measurable improvement in lung capacity related to the subjective feeling of improved stamina in those students practicing qigong breathing techniques. The older students apparently realized the greatest benefit. Their resultant lung capacities were much greater than their age- and height-matched controls (Fig. III). This may reflect that an older student initially has a smaller lung capacity than a younger student. Between the ages of twenty and seventy-one, in the general population, there is a loss of at least 30-35% of the lung capacity, the equivalent of having one-third of the total lung mass surgically removed (West, 1977). However, this "lost" capacity is apparently not lost forever. After they practiced qigong breathing techniques, the lung capacity of the older and younger students were not statistically different (Fig. II). Interestingly, even the younger students demonstrated a significant increase in lung capacity. This indicates that there is considerable room for improvement even in the younger student.

Unlike a machine, in the human body, specific organs, joints and tissues become more efficient, more flexible or more supple with increased use (in the right manner). Qigong breathing promotes a remarkable increase in the lung capacity. Whether the increase in lung capacity reflects an increase in the chest wall size or an increase in flexibility of the lung tissue itself can not be determined from this study. One intriguing possibility is that qigong breathing may increase the usable lung volume. For example, in normal breathing, a human will exchange about 25% of the total lung volume (West, 1977). A whale, however, can exchange greater than 90% of its total lung volume. Qigong breathing may train the student to tap into this large lung volume reserve with every breath, to become more efficient in breathing. Again, this study cannot answer this hypothesis.

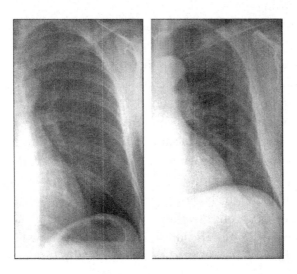

Left: A thirty year old male. Right: A seventy-six year old male.

X-rays comparing the left lung of a young adult male with that of an elderly male. The reduction of lung capacity is largely due to the effects of aging. However, this common tendency for the lungs to progressively decrease in function can be beneficially impeded by regular practice of qigong breathing exercises.

As with all scientific studies, more questions are raised than answered. Would breathing forms in other martial art styles compare favorably with those taught in the Chung Moo style martial art? How fast do qigong breathing techniques increase lung volume? Could qigong breathing movements reverse the severe lung damage from emphysema and cystic fibrosis? How long do the benefits last after stopping qigong breathing? What other organ systems does qigong breathing affect? Preliminary blood pressure studies on students practicing qigong breathing indicate that circulation is also favorably influenced (data not published). It is clear that martial art training and the study of medicine both seek answers to the same questions to understand how the human body works. The combination of martial arts and medicine is exciting in that new insights into how the human body works may be found.

Bibliography

Cheng, Stephen T. (1978). *The book of internal exercises.* San Francisco: Strawberry Hill.

China Sports Magazine. (1985). *The wonders of qigong: A Chinese exercise for fitness, health and longevity.* Los Angeles: Wayfarer.

Eisenberg, David. (1985). *Encounters with qi: Exploring Chinese medicine.* New York: Norton.

Hubbard, R., McElvaney, N., Sellers, S., Healy, J., Czerski, D., and Crystal, R. (1989). Recombinant DNA-produced alpha 1-antitrypsin administered by aerosol augments lower respiratory tract anti-neutrophil elastase defenses in individuals with alpha 1-antiptrypsin deficiency. *Journal of Clinical Investigation,* 84, 1349-54.

Leiner, G., Abramowitz, S., Small, M., Stenby, V., and Lewis, W. (1963). Expiratory peak flow rate. Standard values for normal subjects. Use as a clinical test of ventilary function. *American Review of Respiratory Diseases,* 8, 644-48.

Maliszewski, M. (1992). Medical, healing and spiritual components of Asian martial arts. *Journal of Asian Martial Arts, 1*(2), 25-56.

Massey, P., and Thorner, E. (1992). Personal testimonials gathered from students practicing the Chung Moo style of martial art.

chapter 6

Cultivating the Elixir Field with Sinmoo Hapkido's Danjun Breathing

by Sean Bradley, B.S.

Beginning students practice Danjun Breathing before starting class.
Photos courtesy of Lorene Ledesma, Jeff Hazen, and Suen Sohn.

Introduction

In 1984, Grandmaster Ji Han-jae created Sinmoo Hapkido and introduced his art to the world. Though there is no exact English translation, *Sinmoo* simply translates as "higher mind martial art" (*sin* = higher mind; *moo* = martial art). *Hapkido* means, "the way of coordinating/harmonizing energy. With a strong emphasis on mental and spiritual development, Sinmoo Hapkido moves beyond the basic physical techniques of traditional Korean Hapkido and into a realm of training that involves all aspects of the self. In addition to the sound physical techniques found in all forms of Hapkido, Sinmoo Hapkido teaches a spiritual philosophy and a wide-range of mental exercises.

With numerous breathing and meditation exercises, Sinmoo Hapkido shifts the focus from the multitude of external kicking and joint locking techniques for which Hapkido is known, and places it on internal training and ki development. The first of these internal exercises is Danjun Breathing (DJB).

The *danjun* (Chinese, *dantian*: *dan* = cinnabar; *tian* = field) is a physiologic location where ki accumulates, often referred to as the Elixir Field. Though not an anatomical structure, it is physiologic region of energy accumulation and consolidation. Most martial arts systems recognize three danjuns in the body. The first is located in the midbrain at the level of the eyes. The second danjun is located within the heart the level of the acupuncture point ren-17. The third is located in the lower abdomen. The first two have to do with mental and spiritual development and ki is moved to these areas only for immediate use. Ki is not stored at the upper and middle danjuns. The lower danjun is likewise involved in mental and spiritual development, but is also used for physical development. This is where ki can not only be consolidated and used immediately, but also can be stored and accumulated.

For basic exercises such as DJB, only the lower danjun is used so that ki can be accumulated and stored in order to perform other exercises or for physical exercise. The upper and middle danjuns are typically only used when there is adequate ki already accumulated in the lower danjun. Since the lower danjun is the only one used in DJB, I will use the word danjun to refer only to the lower danjun from now on.

Danjun Breathing is one of many ki development exercises found in the martial arts. In the same tradition as qigong and taijiquan, its foundation is firmly rooted in the Five-Phase Theory used in Traditional Chinese Medicine (TCM) and acupuncture. DJB is not simply a breathing exercise, as it is often times taught, but rather a deep meditation technique that aims at moving and controlling ki within the body. The use of the ki that is gathered and harnessed then depends on the needs of the practitioner. Some of the common uses are to strengthen the body and organs, speed healing, sharpen the mind, warm-up before exercise, aid in spiritual growth, and be applied physically in self-defense situations.

Explanation

The goal of DJB is to effectively mobilize and move ki to specific parts of the body. To do this involves generating ki, consolidating it to a specific area, and then moving it to the desired location. Generated ki is a combination of hereditary constitution, food and water intake, sunshine exposure, and oxygen intake.

Once you generate ki in the body, you will move it to the danjun. Here, you can bring together the ki that is throughout the body to a single point for focused use. Only after enough ki is gathered and brought together will you be able to use it. The exact location of this ki consolidation point in the danjun will vary slightly from person to person because of the variables in each individual's constitution. Grandmaster Ji says that it is approximately the same as the width across their index, middle, and ring fingers. The depth is approximately two inches below the body's surface at this point, but expands outward

75

as more ki converges. According to Boonchai Apichai, qigong instructor at Bastyr University, the danjun is three finger-widths below the umbilicus, and three finger-widths directed into the body. From this point, a three finger-width radius extends to form a sphere. This sphere in the lower abdomen is the danjun. Anteriorly, the acupuncture point ren-6, known as the "sea of qi," corresponds to the danjun. Ren-6 lies on the *ren* or conception vessel. Posteriorly, the sphere extends in a cone-like fashion to a point just below the spinous process of the second lumbar vertebrae at du-4 on the *du* or governing vessel.

Location of Danjun

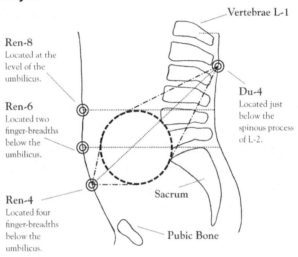

Vertebrae L-1

Ren-8
Located at the level of the umbilicus.

Ren-6
Located two finger-breadths below the umbilicus.

Du-4
Located just below the spinous process of L-2.

Ren-4
Located four finger-breadths below the umbilicus.

Sacrum

Pubic Bone

This diagram shows one possible location of the danjun. This is the area where ki is accumulated for use throughout the body. Depending on development and health, the actual diameter can be larger or smaller. Using acupuncture meridians, the ren points on the front of the body are associated with the conception vessel and the du point on the posterior aspect of the body is on the governing vessel. The danjun lies at a point between the acupuncture points du-4 and ren-4 at approximately the level of ren-6. It lies directly on the midline approximately three finger-breadths below the umbilicus. *Illustration courtesy of Sean Bradley.*

In Hapkido, the danjun is the collecting, combining, and dispersing point for ki. The process is the same in acupuncture and qigong systems where ki is brought together from other areas and collected at this point. From here, we can use ki for a wide variety of functions that will depend entirely on the practitioner and their goals for the exercise.

Preparation

As with any meditative exercise, your surroundings can drastically influence the effectiveness of the technique. Finding the appropriate environment can sometimes be as important as the technique itself.

A quiet place outdoors that receives good sunlight is the ideal location for any ki developing technique. Weather and other environmental factors should not influence your training, but for most people it can be too much of a distraction to properly practice DJB. If this is the case, a consistent and controlled indoor environment might be best. An indoor location should be quiet and without distractions. It needs to be well-ventilated, and ideally get adequate sunlight.

During a 24-hour period, there are twelve hours that are Yin and twelve hours that are Yang. At midnight, darkness, which is Yin, has reached its apex, and begins to turn into light. As the night moves from darkness to the light of sunrise, Yang is taking over. Thus, the Yang period begins at midnight and goes until noon. 5am to 7am is the highest Yang time of day. It will reach its peak at this time of day, and then gradually decline until noon, when Yin will begin to take over again. The day gradually becomes more Yin, until 5pm to 7pm when Yin reaches its peak and begins to decline. At midnight, Yang begins to take over once again. This cycle repeats each day.

There are three times of day that Grandmaster Ji recommends practicing DJB regularly. Before sunrise, noon when the sun is highest, and sunset are all important energy times of day that are perfect for mobilizing ki within your body.

When Yang reaches its peak in the morning, you should exercise. This is the time where the body has the most energy for activity and movement. Perform DJB before exercising in order to generate ki to warm-up the body and use it for the physical activity. The complete body warm-up that takes place in DJB will help you be better prepared for a workout both mentally and physically.

From 11am to 1pm, Yang is changing to Yin. This is a time for relaxing and permitting the body to slowly transition. Practice DJB at this time to generate ki for healing and calming. Ideally, you should perform this exercise just before taking a short nap.

In the evening from 5pm to 7pm, Yin is at its peak. This is the time where the body is best prepared for resting and digesting food. Practice DJB at this time to generate ki to strengthen the organs before eating dinner.

In correlation with the time of day, it is important to have the sun to your back while practicing DJB, especially when practicing outdoors. The back side of the body is the Yang side, and while our back is toward the sun, our "body becomes charged" in much the same way a solar panel becomes charged by the sun. The opposite effect happens when you face your front, or Yin side of the body, toward the sun. This will tend to sap your strength and the benefits of DJB will not occur.

Elevation is another important consideration as it is necessary to take into account your body's ability to effectively absorb and bind oxygen. Grandmaster Ji recommends performing DJB between the altitudes of 2,000 feet and 6,000 feet to put the body in the optimal situation for spiritual meditation. Any higher than 6,000 feet, the unacclimatized individual risks oxygen deprivation.

Body Positioning

With the head and eyes directly forward, stand with your feet slightly wider than shoulder width apart. Your back should be straight, with shoulders slightly pulled back to compensate for the common tendency to roll the shoulders forward and "hunch over." Arms will have a slight bend of approximately 130 degrees at the elbow.

Front view of Master Egil Fosslien, Grandmaster Ji Han-jae, and Master Sean Bradley practicing Danjun Breathing.

Keep your head balanced on three planes. The vestibular system that controls balance and equilibrium is located within the inner ear. The semicircular canals, the utricle, and the saccule make up the vestibular system and are lined with hairs and filled with fluid called endolymph. As your body moves, the fluid flows in different directions causing the hairs to bend. As the hairs bend it triggers a nerve impulse or action potential, which goes to the brain, which then interprets the movement.

The utricle and saccule are the otolith organs found within the ear and measure linear acceleration (i.e. anterior/posterior and elevation/depression). The utricle measures tilt of the head as well as anterior/posterior movement and should remain stationary during DJB. The saccule measures elevation and depression and is the only part of the vestibular system that should move during DJB. There will be a slight rise and fall as your knees bend and extend.

The semicircular canals measure angular acceleration on three planes. Pilots call these three planes pitch, roll, and yaw. Pitch is the flexion and extension motion—nodding your head "yes" or up and down. Keeping your nose and chin in line will prevent pitch. Your nose and chin should form a line that, if extended from the tip of the nose straight down, will intersect perpendicularly with the floor. A common mistake in DJB practice is to have the head tilted back with both the chin and nose raised slightly. Roll is the lateral rotation or lateral bending. This is the motion where you bring your ear toward your shoulder. To prevent this in DJB, your ears should form a parallel plane to the floor.

Yaw is rotation on the horizontal plane or shaking your head "no." The majority of the rotation takes place at the atlanto-axial joint where the spine at the first cervical vertebrae (C1), the atlas, sits atop the second cervical vertebrae (C2), the axis. The atlas sits atop and rotates around the bony prominence on the axis known as the dens. In order to prevent yaw, your eyes should remain straight forward with even distance from the midline. A line should run directly up your spine, and if continued should pass midway between your eyes.

Slight motion in any of the planes may cause you to "lose your balance," and your brain will have to react to regain it. Though this can be very subtle, even the tiniest of head movements may cause you to continually lose your balance. Though you may not notice any movements, if your brain is constantly working to balance, you are not able to work on ki development, because your mind is constantly diverting its focus.

Head balance is important to achieve optimum ki flow through the body.
Yaw – Eye balance. Pitch – Nose and chin balance. Roll – Ear balance.

Breathing

Breathe through your nose in DJB. This allows the small hairs called vibrissae and the mucous lining to filter and warm the air before it enters the bronchi and lungs. Your mouth does not do as good of a job cleaning the air since it lacks this filtering mechanism. Breathing only through the nose will prevent many of the airborne allergens, toxins and other particles from entering the airways.

The breathing cycle for DJB is as follows: inhale for eight seconds, hold for eight seconds, press for four seconds, and exhale for eight seconds. The long inhalation allows for sufficient warming or cooling of the air so that the airway is not shocked from a drastic change in temperature. The holding and pressing cycles allow for pushing and moving ki to different parts of the body. The slow, controlled exhalation allows for enhanced control and strengthening of the body.

In normal quiet inspiration, what Grandmaster Ji calls, "low stomach breathing," the diaphragm contracts and moves inferiorly and flattens out. As the diaphragm extends downward, the thoracic cavity expands. This causes the pressure in the lungs to drop and air outside to flow in.

The longer and slower the breath in, the more inflated the lungs become. As air flows in, the alveoli or alveolar sacs that make up the lungs fill with air. As they fill, they expand and stretch. Slow inhalation not only allows more alveoli to fill with air, but it will let them do so in a more controlled manner. This slow stretch will cause less strain on the epithelial cells that line the interior of the alveoli.

In addition to lung health, this deep contraction tends to strengthen the diaphragm and increases its efficacy. Shinmoo Hapkido postulates that, because the diaphragm is a skeletal muscle just like the biceps in the arm, the slow controlled contraction will increase its strength and endurance in the same way that weight lifting can benefit the arms. In slow and quiet inspiration, we also use the external intercostal muscles that connect the ribs to one another. They help expand the thorax laterally and anteroposteriorly by raising the rib cage and lifting the sternum. The more efficient the diaphragm becomes the less these muscles are used and the less obvious breathing becomes.

Quiet expiration should not actively use any willful tensioning of stomach muscles, but should only be a natural recoil of the lungs. The alveolar sacs that make up the lung tissue are elastic structures much like a balloon. Once the lungs are full, the alveoli will recoil, snapping back to their relaxed position and pushing air out of the lungs.

Controlled expiration however, uses the diaphragm and abdominal muscles and allows for slow and limited recoil. Using this slow, controlled breathing, you strengthen the diaphragm by not letting it simply snap back into place, but rather provide a negative tension on the relaxation phase. You also strengthen the abdominal muscles by tensing and contracting them as you exhale. Having stronger and more toned abdominal muscles will provide for better protection of the internal organs, the danjun, and the solar plexus.

Cycles

There are eight breathing cycles in DJB. This ties directly in with the five-phase theory in Traditional Chinese Medicine (TCM). The five-phases or elements in TCM are wood, fire, earth, metal, and water. Each of these elements is associated with two main organs in the body. For each element, there is a Zang organ and a Fu organ. The Zang organs are associated with Yin and the Fu organs are associated with Yang. The five primary Zang organs are the solid organs that are responsible for storing pure ki. These organs are the liver, heart, spleen, lungs, and kidneys. The five Fu organs are responsible for transmitting water and food without storing them. The Fu organs are small intestine, large intestine, gall bladder, stomach, and urinary bladder.

Element	Zang Organ	Fu Organ	Color	Tissue	Emotion
Fire	Heart	Sm. Intestine	Red	Vessel	Joy
Metal	Lung	Lg. Intestine	White	Skin / Hair	Grief
Wood	Liver	Gall Bladder	Green/Blue	Tendon	Anger
Earth	Spleen	Stomach	Yellow	Muscle	Worry
Water	Kidney	Bladder	Black	Bone	Fear

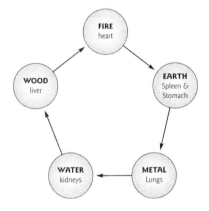

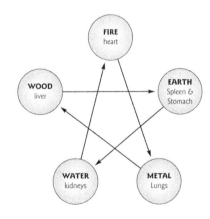

The Generating Cycle

This cycle is for the development of ki in the body. It is not used in Danjun Breathing, but is part of the daily cycle of respiration which occurs on its own.

The Controlling Cycle

This is the cycle followed in Danjun Breathing, where the practitioner begins directing ki to the left side of the heart and ends at the right kidney.

The five elements form one another in a generating or inter-promoting cycle. Wood can burn, giving fire. Fire creates ash, which is earth. Earth processes create various metals. When you smelt metals, you create steam or water. Plants need water in order to grow and produce wood. Rather than the generating cycle, DJB focuses on the interacting or controlling cycle. In this cycle, fire can shape metal, metal can cut wood, wood holds the earth in place, earth diverts and holds water, and water puts out fire. Our body takes control of the generating part of the cycle, but through DJB, we can control the ki that it develops, and use it for whatever we need.

While practicing DJB, focus on the Zang organs. The Fu organs deal with food and water movement and are therefore not relevant to DJB. The only exception to this is the focus on the stomach in addition to the spleen during the sixth breathing cycle. Along with the spleen and lungs, the stomach is one of the sources of ki and is essential in its formation.

In summary, the cycle of eight breaths includes directing the ki to the heart, lungs, liver, stomach/spleen, and kidneys. Practicing DJB in this order helps to control the ki that our body is building and directs it to certain areas in need.

The reason for doing eight cycles instead of only five is due to the paired organs. For the heart, there are two cycles because of the left and right sides of the heart involved in the systemic and pulmonary circulation. There are two cycles for the lungs and two cycles for the kidneys because there are two organs. Thus, the entire cycle is with two breaths for the heart, one breath for each lung, one breath for the liver, one breath for the combined stomach/spleen, and one breath for each of the kidneys.

In the cycles where the organ is paired, it is important to start on the left side. This has to do with the heart chambers. In the left side of the heart, there is oxygenated blood from the lungs that is nourishing to the body. In the right side of the heart, there is deoxygenated blood that needs to go to the lungs to get more oxygen. By starting on the left side when doing this exercise, we allow the nourishment to fill our body and then build. To start on the right side could be potentially dangerous because without the energy from the oxygenated blood we risk not having enough energy to adequately perform the exercise and may even cause more damage.

More important than blood flow is the relationship between Yin and Yang. The left side of the body is the Yang side of the body and the right, Yin. In the same way you need a match to ignite fuel-soaked charcoal, Yang is necessary to initiate Yin. The Yang, being the active side, needs to proceed the passive Yin side, and is therefore first in the breathing cycles. Grandmaster Ji alludes to this by teaching to use the left for generating and the right side for application.

1) Left side of the heart, 2) Right side of the heart, 3) Left lung,
4) Right lung, 5) Liver, 6) Spleen (stomach), 7) Left kidney, 8) Right kidney.

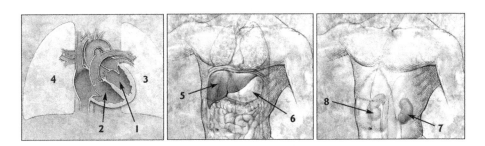

In Danjun Breathing, eight breath cycles constitute a complete
exercise. Each breath corresponds to one of the eight organs.

Technique

Beginning in a relaxed position, slowly inhale through your nose for eight
seconds. As you inhale through your nose, close your mouth and press your
tongue to the roof of your mouth. Doing this joins the ren or conception
vessel that runs up the front of the body and ends at the tip of the tongue to
the du or governing vessel that runs up the body's dorsum, over the head, and
ends in the roof of the mouth. This completes a meridian circuit known as the
microcosmic cycle that permits even and efficient flow of ki through the core
of the body. Be sure to maintain this tongue contact throughout the entire
exercise. Breath in slowly, being sure not to make the air hot or cold. Breathe
deeply and imagine letting the air flow to your danjun and not simply to your
chest.

At the end of your inhalation, relax into your feet and bring your hands,
with palms facing each other and fingers spread, to your hip level approximately one inch from your body. Your hands should be in the "Live Hand" or
"Hands Alive with Ki" position. Spread your fingers and thumb wide. Bend
your knuckles slightly while keeping your palms in a parallel position. Keeping
your face calm and relaxed, hold your breath for eight seconds. As you do this,
direct the ki that you just generated (by bringing oxygen into your body)
toward the danjun area.

When the holding phase is complete, move into the press phase. Clench
your molars tightly together, and bear down as if you were having a bowel
movement and squeeze your anal sphincter shut. Attempt to roll your feet
inward as you contract against the floor and tense your legs. Squeeze your
shoulder blades together and use your back muscles to squeeze your arms toward

your body while you contract your biceps and forearms in order to hold them in place. All of these contractions should be isometric and your body should not move. As you press for four seconds visualize the ki that you have accumulated into your danjun compressing into a tiny ball. Take the ki from a diffuse glob of energy to a small, marble-sized, concentrated ball.

Grandmaster Ji Han-jae demonstrates the proper "Live Hand" position.

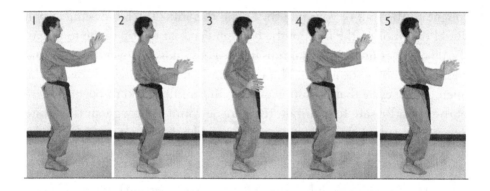

Lateral View of body motion during Danjun Breathing.
• Breathing in (1-3) • Holding & Pressing (3) • Breathing out (3-5).

Breathe out slowly for eight seconds through your nose. Keep your mouth clenched and body tense. Slowly bring your hands up from your hip level pivoting from your shoulders to raise your arms until your fingertips are at eye level. Do not bend your arms further; but rather, keep the slight 130-degree bend that you began with. As you raise your arms, visualize taking the ki from your danjun and directing it to various parts of your body. Initially you will want to practice directing the ki to each of the corresponding organs for the eight cycles in order to strengthen each of these organs. With more experience, directing the ki to the hands is an effective way to generate power for strikes, escapes, and healing. For your own injuries, you can direct the concentrated ki to the area in need to help speed and enhance recovery.

With Danjun Breathing practice, a variety of escapes, throws, and joint-locks can be applied using direction of ki with proper body mechanics.

1-a-b) GM Ji Han-jae demonstrates "live hand" application applying an arm bar.

2a) The "Live Hand" and ki movement is used to escape from a wrist grab.
2b) By controlling ki flow to the hands it is possible to throw an attacker.

85

Conclusion

As a seemingly simple breathing exercise, DJB requires stamina, discipline, and physical and mental control in order to perform correctly and experience the benefits of practice. DJB is a technique that takes years of practice to do effectively, but the results are worth the training. The focused breathing and ki movement through inhalation, holding, pressing, and exhalation enhance mental concentration, boost physical strength and endurance, and most importantly, fine-tune ki control. To be able to effectively mobilize and move ki in your body can have profound effects in a martial artists' training as well as in every day activities.

For martial arts training, moving ki can increase strength and power in given techniques. Ki can help muscles work more effectively to form protective barrier against strikes as well as well as move to areas of injury to help facilitate healing. In everyday life, proper ki movement helps control respiration and digestive functions, which can help one relax, make better use of oxygen intake, and assist in proper food digestion.

Notes

1 Many people may be more familiar with the Chinese translation or pronunciation of qi. This is the same concept, but I have chosen to use the Korean pronunciation because of Sinmoo Hapkido's Korean background.

2 There are actually six Zang organs and six Fu organs. The pericardium is the extra Zang organ and the Triple Heater (*San Jiao*) is the additional Fu organ. The pericardium is the outer protective covering of the heart, and the San Jiao is the connective tissue matrix that connects the internal organs. They are associated with the fire element, and are most often grouped together with the heart and small intestine in the Five-Element Theory.

Bibliography

Apichai, B. (Fall 2005). Qigong I. Classroom lecture. Kenmore, WA: Bastyr University.

Deadman, P., Al-Khafaji, M., and Baker, K. (1998). *A manual of acupuncture.* Hove, England: Journal of Chinese Medicine Publications.

Ding, W. (Fall 2002). Traditional Chinese medicine fundamentals. Classroom lecture. Kenmore, WA: Bastyr University.

Ellis, A., Wiseman, N., and Boss, K. (1991). *Fundamentals of Chinese acupuncture.* Brookline: Paradigm Publications.

Ji, Han-jae (2005, October 15). Personal interview. Puebla, Mexico.

Ji, Han-jae (2005, September 23-25). Sinmoo Hapkido Seminar, Connecticut Sinmoo Hapkido. South Windsor Community Center, Connecticut.

Ji, Han-jae (2003, March 24-26). International Sinmoo Hapkido Master/ Instructor Seminar. Kenmore, WA: Bastyr University.

Ji, Han-jae (2002, December 25). Personal interview. Trenton, New Jersey.

Mitchell, R. (2005 Fall). Meridians and points I. Classroom lecture. Kenmore, WA: Bastyr University.

Pak, T. (2002, December 25). Personal interview. Trenton, New Jersey.

Acknowledgment

The author would like to thank Grandmaster Ji Han-jae and Master Egil Fosslien for their help and for appearing in the pictures used for this chapter. Also, special thanks to the following students for appearing in additional pictures used in this article: Yi-Pei Lin, Steve Matthewson, Jamie Drain, Tennyson Towl, Melissa Mokarzel, Lorene Ledesma, Kim Iller, Courtney Coale Carag, and Robin Terranella.

chapter 7

Hapkido's Defenses
Against Multiple Opponents
by Marc Tedeschi, B.A.

Introduction

Hapkido is a Korean martial art which emerged in the mid-twentieth century and quickly grew to become an international style. Its founders created the art by selectively fusing a wide range of existing martial skills, with new innovations. As a result, Hapkido possesses one of the most complex, unique, and varied arsenals of self-defense techniques to be found in any martial art. These techniques encompass all major martial skills: strikes, kicks, blocks, avoiding movements, holds, joint locks, chokes, throws, breakfalls, tumbling, ground fighting, weapons, meditation, and healing. Like many Asian martial arts, Hapkido emphasizes the unification of body, mind, and spirit; the perfection of human character; social responsibility; and appropriate use of force. Unlike most martial arts, Hapkido utilizes more than 1100 core techniques, which are intuitively modified or combined to create thousands of variations. Self-defense techniques are characterized by a constant flow of striking, blocking, holding, and throwing techniques. Constant motion and fluid circular movements are designed to blend with an opponent's force. Tactics often alternate between highly aggressive and defensive modes, with power being generated through use of one's entire body. Internal energy development is fundamental to all training, leading to increased health and greater efficiency in self-defense techniques.

The following material will provide the reader with a brief picture of a very diverse martial art by presenting a small sample of Hapkido's defenses against multiple opponents. These defenses span all manner of situations and incorporate an extremely broad range of martial skills. Consequently, this chapter well represents the breadth and scope of this fascinating martial art. Most of the basic principles outlined at the beginning of this chapter can be adapted to virtually any martial art style.

Multiple Opponents in the Real World

Defending against multiple attackers can be compared to playing chess games against several opponents simultaneously. You must divide your mental and physical resources among all your opponents, while each of them must only concentrate on you. It is not hard to see who is at a disadvantage.

Before proceeding further, it is important to dispel some common misconceptions regarding self-defense against multiple opponents. In movies and television, it is common to see a single martial arts expert easily dispatching multiple attackers, with a variety of strikes, kicks, holds, and throws. The hero's superior skill devastates an army of formidable opponents, while he or she remains unscathed. While this is theoretically possible, one must recognize that movies are not reality. If you are fighting more than one opponent, the odds are against you. Even if you are a much better fighter, you will probably lose or at least suffer significant injuries. The myth of the invincible warrior overcoming overwhelming odds is exactly that, a myth. In reality, confronting multiple opponents is one of the most complex, stressful, and dangerous self-defense situations you are ever likely to encounter. If weapons are involved, then things will become even more difficult.

• • •

BASIC PRINCIPLES

Hapkido is a composite martial art combining all the major martial technique categories. Consequently when defending against multiple attackers, you should be prepared to counter with avoiding movements, strikes, kicks, holds, or throws—seizing any opportunity you are presented with. Generally, there are many different tactics and approaches for dealing with multiple attackers. The following basic principles apply to most situations and will help to offset your disadvantage.

Hapkido is a composite martial art combining all major martial technique categories: avoiding movements, strikes, kicks, holds, or throws. This photo shows the author executing a simultaneous wrist lock and side kick. Applying several techniques at the same time is a hallmark of Hapkido.

1) Run Away
The best way to deal with a bad situation is to avoid it. Running away is always your first choice. Look for exits that allow you to remove yourself from the area of conflict: run up a stairway, run into a busy public place, barricade yourself in another room, etc. This is not a sign of cowardice, but of intelligence. Being brave will not change the balance of power, so if you don't have to fight—then don't. Avoiding the conflict will also greatly simplify your life: there are no legal issues to address; you will not need to explain excessive or deadly use of force on your part; you have not risked your life; and you are no worse off, perhaps even wiser.

2) Give Them What They Want
If muggers want your wallet, give it to them. Nothing in it is worth risking your life or your health for. Even if you win a fight (seriously injuring or humiliating your attackers), this does not mean it is over. They may return days, weeks, or even months later (with their friends), seeking revenge. You may now be dealing with a far more serious situation than the one you were originally involved in.

Finger-locks are one of the strongest forms of submission holds, and require very little force if properly done. In this photo, finger-locks force two opponents to collide as they fall.

3) Distract and Deceive

Talk, yell, ask questions, or knock things over. Engage in unusual or eccentric behavior. Do anything that causes your opponents to be confused or hesitant, or hinders their concentration. Distractions increase the chances that your initial responses will be successful. If your attackers are under the influence of alcohol or narcotics, confusing behavior can often be very effective. You can also try to camouflage your skills or appear helpless. Sometimes cowering stances can be used to lull your opponents into a false sense of confidence. Sometimes the opposite tactic may be effective. For example, bragging about your skills or adopting a ferocious posture may cause your opponents to back down. It could also have the opposite effect, if they take it as a challenge or an insult. Every situation is different and you must make the decisions you feel are most appropriate at that moment.

4) Attack First

If you believe a fight is inevitable, attack first before your opponents are ready. Target the largest person or the leader. Attack vital points and try to cause serious injuries. The purpose of this is to remove people from the conflict and create fear in the minds of the other attackers. If they are leaderless, or fear they will be similarly injured, they may abandon their attack. When initiating an attack to several opponents at close range, alternate your attack between different attackers.

5) Use One Opponent Against Another

Use footwork and movement to maneuver your opponents into awkward positions, causing them to clash or get in each other's way. When executing throws, try to toss one attacker into another. You can also secure one person by using a joint lock or choke, and use them as a shield against the other attackers. If you must abandon your "shield," finish the hold with a break or dislocation, so they cannot continue to fight.

6) Keep Moving and Maintain Distance

A moving target is much harder to hit, grab, or hold than a stationary one. Keep moving away and try to maintain a safe distance. Your attackers must be within a certain range in order to execute specific techniques. If you can manage to stay outside their range, then they cannot hit or grab you. If you can make them take chances or awkward steps, you will increase your chances for a successful counter. Use a blend of spinning, turning, ducking, slipping, and stepping actions to maintain motion. *Constant movement* is a fundamental Hapkido principle found in all its forms of self-defense, and nowhere is it more important than against multiple attackers.

> Important principles: attack first, keep moving, and use one opponent against another. A–C: Defender attacks first by striking three opponents simultaneously. D: Defender cross-steps forward and strikes a pressure point on the face. E–F: Defender pivots 270° without stepping, blocks a punch and strikes a pressure point on the throat. G–J: Defender pivots 180° under attacker's arm, twisting and locking his arm behind his back. He then throws one opponent into another, while using the hammer lock to dislocate the shoulder.

7) Look for an Equalizer Weapon

Look for anything that can be used as a weapon to equalize the balance of power: a club, bottle, scissors, knife, or objects you can swing or throw—anything that will help to equalize the confrontation in your favor. Throwing sand, stones, or coins (which you can carry in your pocket), may be of some use in setting up your techniques. If you take a weapon away from someone, use it against the others.

8) Avoid Ground Fighting

In almost all situations, you should avoid using any techniques that will put you on the ground (e.g., sacrifice throws or submission pins). Ground techniques may be very useful against a single attacker; however, against multiple opponents, you will be placing yourself in a highly vulnerable and immobile position against other attackers who are still standing. If you are on the ground, it is very easy for them to kick, stomp, or pile on top of you. If you are knocked to the ground, try to return to a standing posture as quickly as possible.

Hapkido includes many techniques for throwing two opponents simultaneously. These complex skills, which are usually part of master-level training, require speed, timing, and complete blending with the opponents' movements. This permits one to overcome the superior strength of two attackers. Detailed knowledge of anatomy and pressure points is also vital, since this allows one to control one's opponents using much less force. The throws shown above were initiated by applying simultaneous joint locks, combined with strong unbalancing motions.

Practical use of one's environment is an integral part of dealing with multiple opponents. The photos show how Hapkido twin-kicks are employed in this situation. Normally, these aerial kicks require years of training to be executed safely and effectively. However, using the environment or an opponent for support, makes them much easier. Two examples are shown at left: K. Twin Side Kick (vaulting over an injured attacker). L. Overhead Split Kick (forced back onto a tabletop).

9) Respond Intuitively

Respond to situations intuitively. Don't try to plan things out or use pre-arranged defenses. Be ready to modify any technique, based on the needs of the moment. Be quick, decisive, and committed to any action you undertake. Intuitive improvisation is a fundamental long-term objective in all Hapkido training. Nowhere is it more important and difficult, than when defending against multiple opponents.

HAPKIDO FUNDAMENTALS IN BRIEF

There are several important ideas which are fundamental to executing most Hapkido techniques. These concepts are also an integral part of defenses shown on the following pages and are summarized below:

• *Leading* – Leading refers to the act of directing your opponent into a hold by using their own energy against them. This may involve redirecting a strike or charge, or creating an initially deceptive movement that causes your opponent to react by moving in a direction that assists the execution of your technique. Leading movements can be short or long depending on circumstances, and are often executed in the opposite direction in which you intend your opponent to move. For example, if you pull an opponent's arm toward your right, they will often react by pulling to your left. This sets up specific strikes, holds, or throws.

Live-Hand: formation with five fingers spread.

• *Live-Hand* – The term Live-Hand refers to specific hand formations which are used to increase the flow of *ki* (internal energy) into the hands and arms. This increases arm strength and power when most needed, such as during a wrist escape or application of a joint lock hold. Live-Hand techniques involve visualization, breath control, and tensing of the fingers, hands, and arms. The use of a Live-Hand is typically characterized by extending one or more fingers and breathing out as a specific technique is applied.

• *Pressure Points* – Many Hapkido techniques make use of pressure points. These are the same points commonly used in Eastern medicine. On the following pages, points are cited using their standard alphanumeric name (e.g., TW-11).

Typical Techniques
Nineteen typical Hapkido defenses against multiple opponents are shown on the following pages. Defenses are arranged by type of attack (e.g., wrist grabs) The techniques shown are meant to illustrate basic fundamentals, and do not necessarily represent the best possible choices in any given situation. In reality, multiple opponent scenarios vary so widely that no prearranged response will ever adequately serve your needs. Therefore, it is important to train with partners in free-fighting exercises, in which you cultivate your own intuitive responses to a wide variety of situations and body-types.

MULTIPLE OPPONENTS
Four Defenses Against Wrist Grabs

1. Wrist-Lock Throw + Passing Shoulder Lock
Two attackers grab your wrists. Form Live-Hands (A). Circle your right hand outward, up, and over right-attacker's wrist, bending his wrist and elbow. Throw

by driving his locked wrist into his throat, as you lift his chin with your palm. You can also thrust your fingers into the throat at pressure point CO-22 (B–C). Grip left-attacker's right wrist with your right hand and twist it outward. Step behind your left foot with your right foot (D), pivot 270°, and pass his arm over your head. Lever your left hand free and grip his wrist (E). Pull down to lock his shoulder and throw (F).

2. Knee Arm Bar + Forearm Arm Bar

Two attackers grab your wrists. Form Live-Hands. Step forward with your right foot and lead both hands forward to weaken attackers' grips (A). Retract your right foot backward into a Cat Stance. Circle both your hands backward and under attackers' wrists (B). Grip their inner wrists in the "V" between your thumb and index finger (C). Twist and pull their hands down (D). Lock the elbow of opponent on your right with your knee (E). Push down and pin by kneeling on pressure point TW-11, which is located 1.5 to 2 inches above the point of the elbow on the triceps tendon. Lock the elbow of opponent on your left, with your right forearm (F). Force a fall (G).

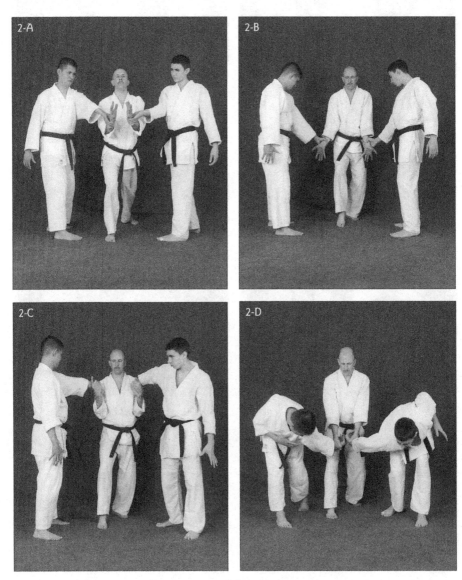

2-E

Detail

2-F

2-G

99

3. Elbow Arm Bar + Scoop Wrist Lock

Two attackers grab your wrists. Form Live-Hands (A). Lead your left hand forward and your right hand backward (B). Reverse direction and circle your hands in opposing directions, around attackers' wrists. Your left hand circles under and over; your right hand circles over and under (C). As your wrists lever free, grip attackers' wrists and twist their arms (D). Apply an Elbow Arm Bar to left-attacker, locking his elbow with your elbow. At the same time, apply a Scoop Wrist Lock to right-attacker, by twisting his wrist forward and up (E–F).

3-D

3-E

3-E
Detail

3-F

101

4. Twin Wrist Nerve Throws

Two attackers grab your wrists. Form Live-Hands with both hands (A). Step forward with your right foot and lead both hands forward to weaken attackers' grips (B). Retract your right foot backward into a Cat Stance. Circle both your hands backward and under attackers' wrists (C). Grip their inner wrists in the "V" between your thumb and index finger. Press your index finger base joints (palm side) into pressure point LU-7 by extending your index fingers (D). Throw by stepping forcefully forward with either foot, as you pull attackers' wrists forward and down (E–F).

This counter requires precise targeting of pressure points, proper leading to set up the throw, and complete sensitivity to your opponents' actions.

LU-7 is located on the thumb-side of the forearm, in a crevice at the inner edge of the radius bone, about 1.5 inches above the wrist crease.

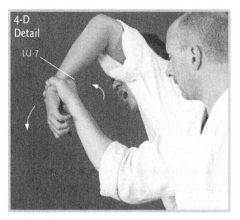

4-D
Detail

LU-7

4-E

4-F

5. Bent Wrist Lock + Scoop Shoulder Lock

Two attackers grab your sleeves near the elbows. Form Live-Hands (A). Circle your hands in opposing directions, around attackers' wrists. Your right hand circles under and over; your left hand circles over and under (B). As their hands become twisted in your sleeves, clamp your elbows closed, trapping their hands in your right inner elbow and left armpit (C). Twist their hands. Rotate your right elbow over right-attacker's bent-wrist; snap down to lock his wrist. At the same time, lock the shoulder of left-attacker by scooping his elbow with your wrist (D–E).

5-C
Detail

5-D

5-D
Detail

5-E

6. Twin Scoop Shoulder Locks

Two attackers grip your sleeves at your shoulders or elbows, with their arms bent (A). Step forward with your right foot. Circle your Live-Hands up and back, striking facial pressure points with your knuckles (B). Continue circling your hands around their arms (C), driving your thumb knuckles or wrists against the sides of their elbows (D). Lock their shoulders by scooping their bent-elbows inward and up, as you trap their wrists in your armpits (E). Step back and lower your body to force falls (F). You can also throw by stepping forward and dropping to one knee.

6-D

6-E

6-E
Detail

6-F

7. Twin Inner-Elbow Arm Bars

Two attackers grab your belt (A). Form Live-Hands and slide your left foot forward. Lift your arms and place your inner elbows against the back of attackers' elbows, just above their joints. Step forcefully forward with your right foot (B). As attackers' arms pull straight, lock or break their elbows by thrusting your inner elbows forward (C). Drive attackers toward each other, forcing their heads to clash. Redirect them to the ground (D). Grip their wrists with your hands and pull up. Wrap your leg over their elbows and press down to lock joints (E–F).

6-A

6-B

6-C

6-D

6-E

6-E
Detail

6-F

7-F
Detail

109

8. Side Kicks + Wrist Nerve Throws

You are seated. Two attackers grab your wrists. Form Live-Hands (A). Lead both hands forward to weaken attackers' grips. Circle both your hands backward and under attackers' wrists. Grip their inner wrists in the "V" between your thumb and index finger. Press your index finger base joints (palm side) into the LU-7 pressure point by extending your index fingers (B). Throw attacker on right by pulling his wrist forcefully down to your left front-corner, as you execute a Right Side Kick to his left knee (C–D). Repeat the same throw to attacker on right (E–F).

8-C
Detail

8-D

8-E

8-F

9. Forearm-to-Leg Throw, Back Fist, Kick

Two attackers grab your wrists. Form Live-Hands (A). Lever both hands free using any wrist escape (B). Throw right-attacker by gripping his left ankle at the SP-6 pressure point with your left hand, as you press his left knee with your right wrist (C–D). Keep your head down to avoid a right falling kick. Target back of knee at points BL-53 or BL-54, side of knee at GB-34, or front of knee at ST-35 or kneecap. Execute a left Back Fist Strike to left-attacker's inner shin at SP-6 or LV-5 (E). Plant both hands, roll onto your left knee, and deliver a right Roundhouse Kick to the groin or head (F). Stand up.

9-C
Detail

SP-6

9-D

9-E

Detail
Hit SP-6

9-F

113

10. Passing Cross Arm Bars (front)

Two attackers grab your wrists. Form Live-Hands (A). Circle both your hands backward and over attackers' wrists (B). Grip their wrists in the "V" between your thumb and index finger. Press the LU-7 pressure points with your base joints. Twist their arms outward as you raise your right knee (C). Pass under right-attacker's arm and pivot 180° (D). Raise your left knee and plant your right knee as you cross the attackers' straight-arms, forcing them to collide. Twist and lever their arms, locking their elbows against each other (E). Lower your body as you throw attackers in opposite directions (F–G).

10-E

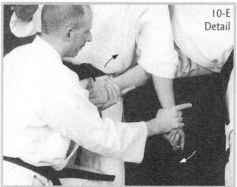

10-E
Detail

10-F

10-G

11. Twin Finger Locks

From a Relaxed Stance (A), step forward with your right foot. Grab one or more fingers on opponents' hands, placing your extended index fingers against their base joints (B). Lock opponents' finger joints by rotating your hands, as you lever their fingertips toward the backs of their hands (C). Turn opponents' palms inward and force them to collide (D). Turn their palms downward and force them to drop (E–F). When applying finger locks, opponents will move in the direction their palms are facing. These are strong holds and can be applied in many ways.

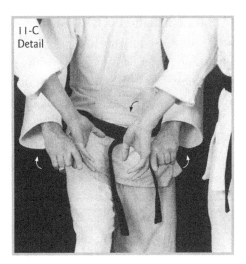

11-C
Detail

11-D

11-E

11-F

117

12. Elevated Palm Lock + Clash

Step forward with your left foot. With your left hand, grab the right hand of left-opponent (A–B). Twist his palm up, locking his wrist backward. Your palm is on the back of his hand. Grip four fingers with your right hand. Lock his finger joints and wrist by levering his fingertips toward the back of his hand. Your palm pushes against his fingers; your fingers pull the base joints (C). Deliver a Reverse Roundhouse Toe Kick to the groin (D). Use the pain of the hold to throw left-opponent into right-opponent (E). If they try to rise, execute a Stamp Kick to clash their heads (F).

Optional Kick: The kick to the groin is optional, and can be used if the attacker at right advances early. Watch your balance, since you are vulnerable to being knocked over. Without the kick, the throw is faster, and balance more stable.

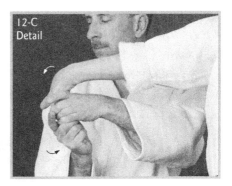

12-C Detail

12-D (optional kick)

12-E

12-F

13. Four Kick Combo

This attack shows how several kicks are fluidly combined into rapid combinations. From a Relaxed Stance, step forward with the left foot (A). Execute a right Roundhouse Kick with the ball or toe of the foot to the groin of left-opponent (B). Without planting your kicking-foot, execute a right Side Kick to the knee or abdomen of right-opponent (C). Plant your right foot and hit him again with a left Back Kick to the head or body (D). Swing your left foot back toward your right foot (swing step) (E), then swing your right leg forward and execute a right Front Heel Kick to the chin of left-opponent (F).

13-A

13-B

13-B
Detail

Hit SP-12 and LV-12

120

14. Side Kick + Elbow Arm Bar

From Fighting Stances, two attackers step forward and execute simultaneous right Lunge Punches (A). As you deflect the punch of attacker on right using a left Inside Parry, execute a left Side Kick to the belly of attacker on left (B–C). Grip right-attacker's wrist and hand with both hands. Plant your left foot toward your right, as you twist his arm inward and pull it straight so the back of his elbow points up. Plant your left elbow over his elbow. Lock or break his elbow by driving your inner elbow down, as you lift his wrist (D–E). Watch for other opponents.

14-C

14-D

14-D
Detail

14-E

123

15. Passing Cross Arm Bars

From Fighting Stances, two attackers step forward and execute simultaneous right Lunge Punches (A). Step backward if needed. With your right foot forward, parry both punches outward (B) as you grip their wrists. Twist the left arm counterclockwise and the right arm clockwise as you circle both arms down and in front (C). Step forward with your left foot. Pass under left-attacker's arm and pivot 180° (D). Cross attackers' twisted straight-arms and lock or break both elbows by levering one against the other (E). Force attackers to collide and fall (F–H).

Arm Bar: The arm bars shown in step E will break both arms and force falls. If right-attacker bends his arm or remains standing, lift and twist his straight-arm close to his body to lock his shoulder and force a fall (G–H).

15-D

15-E (Cross Arm Bars)

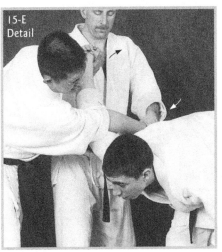

15-E
Detail

15-F

15-G (Shoulder Lock)

15-H

16. Twin Outward Wrist Throws

From Fighting Stances, two attackers step forward and execute simultaneous Lunge Punches (A). Left-attacker punches with his right hand. Right-attacker punches with his left hand. Step backward if needed. Execute Outside Parries with both hands (B) and grab their wrists. Pull them toward you, unbalancing them forward (C). Step forcefully forward and twist their arms as you circle their hands down (D), forward, and up. Lock attackers' elbows on their bellies (E). Lift their twisted-wrists to break their arms or force falls (F).

Note: When executing this hold, one or both opponents will often turn away and lift their elbow(s) to relieve pressure. If this occurs, pull their wrists down as you step back, locking their shoulders and forcing falls (G–H).

16-D

16-E

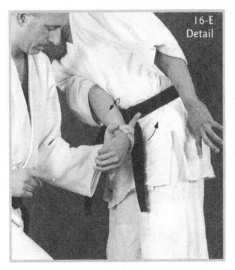

16-E
Detail

16-F

16-G (option, see note above)

16-H

17. Kick-Counter Throws

From Fighting Stances (A), two attackers step in and execute simultaneous kicks. Left-attacker delivers a Roundhouse Kick. Right-attacker delivers a Side Kick (B). Execute Outside Wrap Blocks with both hands, wrapping your arms under their ankles (C). Throw left-attacker by twisting his leg and pulling it to your chest, as you drive your left wrist into his Achilles tendon. At the same time, throw right-attacker by lifting his ankle toward his head (D–E). Based on the degree of leg-twist, you can direct left-attacker under falling right-attacker.

17-D

17-D
Detail

17-E

18. Three Attackers at Front + Sides

Three attackers are in front and on sides. Center-attacker steps forward and grabs your lapel (A). Trap his hand on your chest, gripping his wrist with both hands. Twist his arm and pull it straight (B). Pivot left and break his elbow by driving your elbow down into the joint. At the same time, deliver a right Side Kick to right-attacker as he charges to punch (C). Left-attacker delivers a Side Kick. Step to your left and execute an Outside Wrap Block (D). Lift his leg as you step closer by shuffling your feet. Reap his support-leg with your right leg (E–F).

18-A

18-B

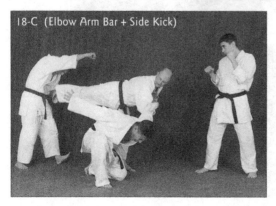

18-C (Elbow Arm Bar + Side Kick)

18-C
Detail

18-D

18-E (Outer Reap Throw)

18-F

19. Four Attackers in Rotation

Four attackers surround you. Attacker behind you applies a Rear Naked Choke (A). Grab his arm, pull it down, and execute a Shoulder Throw, tossing him into right-attacker who is charging in to punch (B). Attacker in front delivers a Side Kick, as left-attacker punches (C). Step lateral to avoid the kick. Execute a Right Outside Hook Throw by deflecting and sweeping the kicking leg upward. At the same time, block the punch, wrap the arm, and scoop the bent-elbow upward as you trap attacker's wrist in your armpit. Dislocate his shoulder and force a fall (D–F).

Acknowledgment

A special thanks goes to Shelley Firth and Frank Deras for the excellent photography, as well as those who appeared with the author in the technical sections: Arnold Dungo, Cody Aguirre, and Michael Mar.

chapter 8

A Few Favored
Sinmoo Hapkido Techniques
by Sean Bradley, B.S.

신무합기도

sin moo hapkido

Where I Learned These Techniques

The basic armbar and the high-section roundhouse kick represent two of the foundational techniques that demonstrate important principles of body mechanics, movement, and technical detail imperative to the art of Sinmoo Hapkido as taught by Dojunim Ji Han-Jae.* I was introduced to both of these techniques in my first class with Dojunim Ji in New Jersey, but have been forced to constantly refine them as I continue to train and better understand the art.

Memorable Incidents Involving These Techniques

The first time Dojunim Ji applied the basic arm bar to me was during my first class with him. I grabbed his wrist and in an instant my face was nearly smashed into the floor. I felt as though my elbow was ripped apart and my wrist was about to explode. The pain was excruciating and there was nothing I could do to fight it.

As for the high-section roundhouse kick, I remember drilling this kick for hours at various times as Dojunim Ji constantly adjusted my footwork, body position, and rhythm of movement. The roundhouse kick is the seventh of the twenty-five basic kicks of Sinmoo Hapkido, and is one of the kicks that give students the most trouble in the beginning. Unfortunately, the most memorable aspect of this technique involves the numerous injuries I have seen people suffer from attempting this kick. Too often, rather than listen to the details of the technique and approach it as a completely new kick, students attempt to perform another style of roundhouse kick, but reach one hand toward the floor, since that is the most obvious feature of how this kick is different. Unfortunately, without all the details, I've seen far too many people drop to the floor grasping a strained hamstring as they mix opposing mechanics.

Tips on Practicing These Techniques

For the basic armbar, the most important tip is not to muscle through the technique, but to use your whole body. It is easy to apply a joint lock to a cooperative opponent, but to apply this technique effectively, you must first unbalance the attacker with the initial step and drop of the body. The side step and drop not only allow you to unbalance the attacker, but also bring the hand to your own midline so you are able to move using your whole body effectively. Pivot the feet and lean forward slightly as you rotate your hips to lock the attacker's arm straight. Continue to control his balance by keeping him on his heels.

It is also important to have the proper graduated handgrip, and to pin the hand to your chest on application so as not to rely on strength, but let body mechanics do the work. Use your body, and also apply leverage to the attacker's thumb to aid in creating some pain compliance, but, more important, keep his arm straight.

The high-section roundhouse kick exists in many forms in many different styles but is unique in its application in Sinmoo Hapkido. This kick utilizes the top of the instep at the ankle or the shin to strike the temple or neck area. The head and torso deliberately drop low in order to allow the leg to go up and kick higher than normal flexibility may allow. Additionally, this motion also drops the head out of the way of a potential strike, and the palm of the hand touches the floor to provide additional balance and push to return to an upright position.

Though most people notice the hand touching the ground and point to this as the major distinguishing factor, it is only a small aspect that sets this technique apart. Dropping the head to allow the leg to get higher without relying solely on flexibility is an important part of performing this kick correctly, but stepping on a forty-five-degree angle and allowing the body to fold at nearly a ninety-degree angle are imperative to ensure optimal power and also decrease the stress on the low back. The regular rhythm is a four-step count that allows the body to move fluidly in a rocking motion that enables the kick to act as a whip.

* *Dojunim* is the honorary title for Ji Han-Jae as the founder of the Korean martial art of Sinmoo Hapkido. Ji is also considered by many to be the founder of modern Hapkido.

Technique 1: Basic Armbar

1a) Spread the fingers of the hand being grabbed creating tension and expanding the tendons of the wrist. **1b)** Take a small side step to the right with the right foot and sink straight down by bending the knees. The right hand moves below the grabbing hand to the outside and then lifts straight, using the legs to stand up. The left hand reaches across and grabs the hypothenar eminence of the attacker's left hand, using the little, ring, and middle fingers to wrap around the meat of the hand below the little finger. The index finger remains straight and pointed. Create a tight seal across the back of the hand by placing the thumb pad at the base of the thumb knuckle. Force should be applied to lock the wrist in a bent position. **1c)** With your left hand, pull the attacker's hand to your chest as the right hand applies pressure forward against his thumb. **1d)** The left foot pivots to the outside, keeping the attacker's hand to the chest and moving the right hand up to three finger widths above the elbow in a tense, active hand position. **1e)** Step forward with the right foot as you apply downward pressure just above the wrist to execute the armbar.

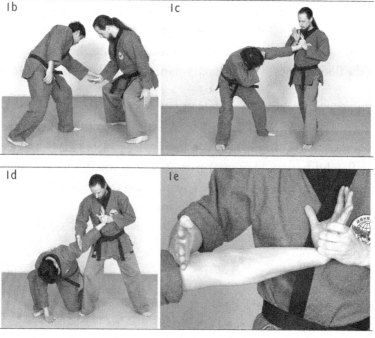

Technique 2: High-Section Roundhouse Kick

2a) Start in a neutral position. **2b)** Step on a forty-five-degree angle to the left. **2c)** The body bends at the waist and the left shoulder begins to drop toward the floor. **2d)** The right knee lifts up and begins to swing in a circular motion to the inside. The left foot pivots slightly on the ball of the foot as the right hip pushes forward and the knee snaps the right foot forward in a whiplike motion. As the foot reaches maximum extension, the left palm touches the floor while the body bends in almost an "L" shape (side view **2e**). The left hand pushes the torso up as the right foot snaps back at the knee and pulls downward toward the floor. The left foot pivots, and when the right foot steps down, the left then steps back to return to the neutral standing posture.

Acknowledgement
Warm thanks to Tiffany Tong
for the photography and to
Alex Mark for helping demonstrate.

index

Made in the USA
Monee, IL
09 July 2024

61540377R00079